Praise for *P*ı

You are in for a challenging
according to Luke led by Mil
Christian leader has furnished h.... ....
story as it bears on our lives today. Be warned: Luke won't leave you comfortable with the way you may follow Jesus now. Yet he will point you to the
One who can enable you to be what God wants you to be.

—E. Glenn Hinson
Professor Emeritus, Baptist Theological Seminary at Richmond

I have been privileged—blessed, actually—to have been a member of a
Baptist church where Dr. Michael A. Smith served as pastor. I have also
been blessed by an abiding friendship with Mike of more than three decades. Mike is a brilliant communicator whose preaching, teaching, pastoral ministry, and congregational leadership have been infused with wisdom,
insight, and a profound understanding of, and love for, Holy Scripture.
While his writing is simple, clear, and direct (much like his preaching), it
is anything but shallow. After reading this book, you too will have a deeper
love for the Gospel of Luke—and for the Jesus who inspired and embodied
the truths of this transformational Gospel.

—David Wilkinson
Executive Director & Publisher, *Baptist News Global*

If you are looking for a polite book to reaffirm your sense of biblical lit-
eracy and justify your limited vision of God's kingdom filled with people
like you, then you better look elsewhere. Here, Mike Smith reminds us
of the radically inclusive, deeply subversive message of Luke's Gospel: one
in which Jesus ran with the wrong kind of people, offended the sincerely
held beliefs of the respectable religious authorities, and lived out God's
preference for loving people over obeying rules. Mike's pastoral voice gently
invites us to hear Luke's ancient stories as our stories here and now, and he
challenges us to find God "working underground" among today's "outsiders." But be warned! For those of us on the "inside," as Mike makes it clear,
the Jesus in Luke's Gospel can not be tamed.

—Bert Montgomery
Author, *A Rabbi & a Preacher Go to a Pride Parade*

Dr. Smith brings his pastoral heart, innovative voice, and stalwart dedication to biblical interpretation to this incredible book. *Preaching the Word: Luke* provides an excellent resource for clergy and laity who take the Scriptures seriously and seek a creative means to proclaim its truths.

—R. Mitchell Randall
Executive Director, *Ethics Daily*

Mike Smith drills down on what separates Luke from the other gospels. "Luke's Gospel tells the good news of Christ to all those considered by others or themselves to be outsiders. Sometimes I call it 'The Outsider's Guide to Jesus.'"

What if today's church took this same approach? Here, readers will recognize the lifelong relationship between a pastor and congregation, his love for Luke's account, and the transformative power of its external focus. Luke's claim on his 1st century audience is evident. In these reflections, its contemporary relevance is undeniable.

—Bill Owen
Center for Healthy Churches

Luke

Preaching the Word

Smyth & Helwys Publishing, Inc.
6316 Peake Road
Macon, Georgia 31210-3960
1-800-747-3016

Library of Congress Cataloging-in-Publication Data

Smith, Michael, 1954 September 1-
Luke / by Michael A. Smith
Macon, GA : Smyth & Helwys Publishing, 2019
Preaching the Word
LCCN 2019004665
ISBN 9781641731249
1. Bible. Luke--Sermons.
2. Bible. Luke--Commentaries.
3. Sermons, American—21st century.
LCC BS2595.54 .S65 2019
DDC 226.4/06--dc23

2019004665

Luke

Michael A. Smith

Also by Michael A. Smith

Mount and Mountain, Volume 1
A Reverend and a Rabbi Talk about the Ten Commandments
with Rami Shapiro

Mount and Mountain, Volume 2
A Reverend and a Rabbi Talk About the Sermon on the Mount
with Rami Shapiro

Beginnings
A Reverend and a Rabbi Talk About the Stories of Genesis
with Rami Shapiro

Dedication

To Bob Byrd and E. Glenn Hinson,

who taught me to take the Scriptures seriously and think for myself,

and to my wife Grace,

whose love for the Scriptures continues to inspire me

Contents

Preface   1

1. The Outsider's Guide to Jesus   3
2. God Remembers   7
3. God and the Maiden   11
4. It's the Little Things   15
5. Zechariah's Finest Hour   19
6. The Multiple Miracles of Christmas   23
7. Temple Stories   27
8. Preparing for Jesus   31
9. The Temptations   35
10. There's Room at the Canvas   37
11. A Meditation on Ministry   41
12. How Will I Draw Others toward Christ?   43
13. Will They Call Us "Friend"?   47
14. A Meditation: Round Pegs in Square Holes   51
15. Luke's Take on the Beatitudes   53
16. Love and Judgment   57
17. A Meditation: Christ Is with Us   61
18. A Sower Goes on Sowing   65
19. What Is Your Name?   69
20. Resetting Our Expectations about Life with Jesus   73
21. The Day After   77
22. Sent Out   79
23. Reshape Your Life   81
24. How to Find Your Focus   85
25. The Shape of Prayer   89
26. Can We See What Is in Front of Us?   93
27. A Self-test   95
28. Live as if There Is a God   99

29. The Woman Who Did Not Fit   101
30. A Meditation: Mustard Seeds and Yeast   105
31. Let's Talk about the Narrow Gate   107
32. Come Home   111
33. Lessons from a Bad Man   115
34. The Lazarus Challenge   117
35. Words for Disciples in the Making   121
36. Jesus and the Lepers   125
37. The Kingdom of God Is Now   129
38. Questions I Ask Myself   131
39. The Man with Everything   135
40. Six Lessons for the Road   137
41. Three Warning Signs of Unhealthy Religion   141
42. Questions   145
43. Why Am I Religious?   149
44. What to Do when the World Falls Apart   153
45. At the Table of Christ   157
46. When Jesus Stood Alone   161
47. "I Shall Die, and Remain Myself": The Death of Jesus   163
48. We Are Easter People   167
49. Walking with Christ   171
50. Open Your Mind   173

Preface

Pastors conduct a running conversation with the biblical text, congregation, God, and themselves. Several times a week, we share some of the results with others in the form of sermons, lessons, meditations, and the like. While we delve into biblical studies, theology, psychology, history, and other disciplines, our focus is on living the new life available in Christ. The materials which comprise this book took shape in the context of the life of Central Baptist Church of Fountain City.

I confess that Luke is my favorite among the four Gospels. I first fell in love with Luke while listening to Frank Stagg give his take on the text. Over the subsequent decades, I've found Luke's insight into Jesus, compassion for the "least of these," insistence on inclusivity, and love of a good story to be invaluable. I enjoy the directness of Mark, the structure of Matthew, and the loftiness of John, but always I return to Luke, the only Gentile among the Gospel writers.

I thank the good people of Central Baptist Church of Fountain City, Knoxville, Tennessee, for their willingness to engage the biblical text and life. They encourage me. I'm grateful for such a congregation. I especially thank my spouse Grace, who encourages me to keep thinking, writing, and ministering in season and out.

The Outsider's Guide to Jesus

Luke 1:1-4

Long ago a child was born to Greek-speaking parents living somewhere in the Roman world, and they named the baby Luke.

Truth to tell, that's all we know about Luke's history before he appears as a traveling companion of Paul. Admitting this is so, I still find myself wondering about Luke's early life. What might have prepared and motivated him to become the kind of person who would write the Gospel of Luke and the Acts of the Apostles?

I suspect the answer lies in a yearning for God.

Mind you, I can't prove it, but I think it likely that Luke came from among the first-century folk called "God fearers." They were Gentiles who had come to admire the ethics of Judaism and sought to honor the God of Abraham, Isaac, and Jacob. Unless they chose to become Jews, God fearers were barred from full participation in Jewish life. Few Gentiles took such a step. A God fearer might be respected by Jewish leaders, contribute funds to the synagogue, and lead a praiseworthy life, but they remained an outsider.

Luke, though, came to know the God who loved both Jew and Gentile. In Christ, Luke found a community (at least Paul's wing of it) who welcomed all those who followed Christ as Lord.

And Luke took up the task of sharing such a Christ with those like him, outsiders who nonetheless yearned for God.

He did his homework. Luke talked with as many of those who had known Jesus as he could find. He probably spoke with Peter, John, and others from among the twelve disciples. I would not be surprised to learn that he interviewed Mary herself and other women who played roles in the life of Jesus. He listened to or read the stories gathered by others. As he did so, Luke discerned that Jesus broke down barriers. The Jesus he discovered moved freely among the rich and poor, the righteous and the unrighteous, the healthy and sick, and men and women.

In Jesus, Luke found the way to God not only for himself but for all persons, no exceptions allowed.

All of which leads to the name of the person to whom Luke addressed his Gospel: Theophilus. The name means "lover of God" or "God lover." Luke addressed his Gospel to all those who loved God. He wrote it to introduce them to Jesus, through whom they might come to know the God who was for them, the God who chose to come and find them, the God who welcomed them.

Luke's Gospel tells the good news of Christ to all those considered by others or themselves to be outsiders. Sometimes I call it "The Outsider's Guide to Jesus."

As we read and ponder Luke, try asking the following questions of the texts:

1. Are there "outsiders" in the story? If so, who are they and why are they "outsiders"? What factors assign them that role and keep them in it?

2. Are there "insiders" in a given story, people assumed by culture or themselves to be "in" with God? If so, who are they and why are they "insiders"? What factors assign them that role and keep them in it?

3. Who benefits from the arrangement in which some are outsiders and some are insiders? What forms do the benefits take?

4. How does Jesus respond to the people in the story, both outsiders and insiders? Does he accept or challenge the situation? Do his followers tend to help or hinder him?

5. Where do you fit into the story? Answering this question may be more difficult than it seems. Use your imagination, be honest, and go with the results. For example, when we come to the Parable of the Loving Father, ask yourself whether you most easily see yourself in the younger brother, the loving father, or the older brother. When you find your answer, you're on your way to discerning what Luke has to tell you through the story.

Somewhere along the way, we'll discover we're all outsiders, all in need of God's grace. Perhaps we will start to grasp Luke's sense of wonder at what God has done through Christ, accept our kinship with all people, tear down the walls we've built between others and ourselves, and enter willingly into God's community.

Why not take for yourself the name of Theophilus as we journey through Luke's Gospel? Who knows? Your life may be changed in such a fashion that it becomes a story in itself, the kind of story in which others find a trustworthy guide to Jesus.

God Remembers

Luke 1:5-25

If you look in most English Bibles, you'll find Luke 1:5-25 preceded by a heading that goes something like this: "The Birth of John the Baptist Foretold."

Such headings are accurate enough, but they may cause us to miss something important to Luke. The story starts with a theme of its own: "God remembers God's promise."

"Where's that?" you wonder. It's encoded in the names of an elderly couple. The husband is named Zechariah, which means "God remembers," and the wife is named Elizabeth, which means "God's promise." For Luke, the story is about the God who remembers God's promise to redeem or rescue the people of God. God's memory of the promises made finds expression through the lives of Elizabeth and Zechariah.

Imagine them as a young couple. Their marriage joined two lines of priestly descent in one household. While not among the upper crust of the priestly families, they enjoyed the respect of their neighbors. They wanted children, of course. Their culture saw children as a mark of God's favor. Zechariah and Elizabeth probably expected to be blessed with many children.

The years passed, and no child came. Tongues began to wag. Extended family members probably asked what sin one of them had committed to result in such a thing. Perhaps Zechariah and Elizabeth questioned their own worthiness.

They continued to do what they knew to do: worship God, care for one another, pray, and tend to their respective duties. By the time old age set in, both had made some kind of peace with their lot in life.

In some ways, their lives mirrored the larger life of Israel. Few if any among the first-century Jews doubted they were God's people, and most knew of God's promise to remember and redeem them. Still, many lifetimes had come and gone since the making of that promise. Some probably thought there was little use in looking for the promise to be fulfilled—at least in their lifetime. Best simply to get on with life as it was.

Certainly, that's what Zechariah was doing the day he went to the temple to fulfill his duty. The last thing he expected was a visit from the angel Gabriel.

Gabriel delivered a message, which paraphrased went like this: "God is about to fulfill his promise to redeem Israel. Your wife Elizabeth will bear a son, who in due time will prepare the way for him who is to come. You will rear him as one dedicated to God, and you will name him John."

Shocked, Zechariah could only ask, "How can this be?" There's a bit of dark humor at play here, for Zechariah surely knew the stories of how God enabled the pregnancies of Sarah, the mother of Isaac, and Hannah, the mother of Samuel. It's one thing to know what God has done for others; it's another thing to imagine God doing something similar in your life.

Gabriel was not amused. The angel sentenced Zechariah to muteness until John's birth. Soon his time on duty was finished, and he returned home.

Shortly thereafter, Elizabeth conceived and went into seclusion for five months. With the evidence growing in her womb, Elizabeth accepted the child as a blessing.

God remembers God's promises. That's the good news with which Luke opens his Gospel, and it's good news to all of us as well. The trick is to live as if Luke got it right.

How do we do so, when life stretches out and the promises continue to go unfulfilled? What if we've fallen into the pattern of living life as we've known it and—honestly—left little room for a surprise from God?

Personally, I long ago fashioned a brief prayer to help me stay open to the possibility of God fulfilling God's promises. It's not the only prayer I pray, but I add it to my other prayers as often as possible. This prayer helps me graft the story of Elizabeth and Zechariah onto the unfolding story of our congregation, the larger church, your lives, and even my life. May it do the same for you.

Help me, Lord, lest I forget that you never forget your world, your church, or me.

I confess I'm often worn down by the grind of life. Many a day I rise from sleep filled not with anticipation for what you might do that day but instead with grim determination to make it through yet another day.

I confess that when I look at your church, I usually see its habitual sins rather than its potential glory. I confess that when I look at the lives of others, I do not always see your image in them, but instead only the evil they do to themselves and others. I confess, too, that I frequently fail to see your image in me.

Help me, O Lord, lest I forget that you never forget your world, your church, or me. Teach me to watch for what you are doing even now.

In the name of your promise made flesh, Jesus Christ, I pray. Amen.

God and the Maiden

Luke 1:26–38

We love the story of God and the maiden, the tale of that day when the angel Gabriel came to Mary, told her God wanted her to conceive and bear and rear Jesus, and waited for her response.

The longer I live with the story, the more I find myself asking two questions. How did the teenager find it in herself to say yes? Is it possible we might say yes to whatever God proposes to do in partnership with us?

What enabled Mary to say yes to God? Four factors came together.

Preparation. Mary lived in a God-centered culture. The stories of God and her ancestors were told and retold in family and worship settings. Synagogue worship and Sabbath observance set the rhythm of her life. Prayers scattered throughout each day reinforced her sense of the presence of God.

Mary's life prepared her to believe God was active in God's world. She knew the stories of a God who visited people to invite them to partner with God in amazing ways, and in each of the stories the person said yes.

Realism. Mary asked, "How can this be, since I am a virgin?" (v. 34). Wrapped up in the question is the realistic characteristic of God's ancient people.

God's chosen people often challenged God. Abraham and Sarah questioned the possibility of people their age having a baby. Moses debated with God at the burning bush. Abraham, Sarah, Moses, Mary, and many others essentially asked the same question: "How can this be?"

Mary had good reasons to raise the question.

She was a virgin, so she had had no opportunity to become pregnant. Even if she conceived and bore a son, she could see no way he might thrive, let alone reign over the house of Jacob. She was a young woman living in a culture that penalized women who become pregnant outside of marriage. In all likelihood, she faced being cut off by her family, rejected by her prospective husband Joseph, and—if matters really got out hand—stoned to death.

There's more. She lived under the rule of someone who already claimed the title "King of the Jews," a man named Herod who had a history of killing real and assumed rivals.

"How can this be?" was a big question that tied together biology, family, religion, society, and politics. "God, how can this be? Given all these factors, how can you hope to accomplish such a thing?"

God through Gabriel answered—more or less—"All things are possible with God. For example, your aged cousin Elizabeth is now six months into an impossible pregnancy. Go see for yourself."

The answer provided Mary a way to satisfy her concern, and it also reminded her of something she already knew. Time and time again, God had chosen ("favored") someone and through that person brought about something thought impossible. Isaac, the exodus from Egypt, the return from exile in Babylon—perhaps these and other stories flitted through Mary's mind.

The answer to Mary's question was that she already knew the answer to the question: all things are possible with God. All she had to do was remember the stories of her people. If she needed additional assurance, she could go and check on Elizabeth for herself!

Choice. Mary came to realize the question was not whether God was at work in God's world or could bring all this to pass. Instead, the question was what would Mary choose to do.

Mary knew the choice was hers to make. All of God's history with God's people distilled down to a single moment with an individual whose response to God determined what would or would not come next.

Her decision mattered.

She made a decision, spoke it aloud, and felt it take hold of her life: "Let it be with me according to your word" (v. 38). Mary said yes.

Consequences. Saying "Yes" was not the end of the matter. Immediately, Mary started to live out her "yes" through consequence after consequence.

She became pregnant. As her body started to change, everything became quite real. She had to deal with her parents, Joseph, and the neighbors.

The consequences kept on coming: a hard journey to Bethlehem and a delivery in a stable; strange folk showing up to see the baby; fleeing to Egypt to escape Herod's murder of the children; dealing with the child

Jesus; Jesus leaving home and taking up his ministry; Jesus dying. The consequences never stopped coming.

Part of the greatness of Mary, the greatness of anyone who says yes to God, is that she chose to live with the consequences.

Let's return to the second question: Is it possible we might say yes to whatever God proposes to do in partnership with us?

Yes.

Mary's story points the way.

Prepare by immersing yourself in the story of God's people, ancient and modern. Start to cultivate a mindset that assumes God is present and at work in God's world. Lay your real questions on the table before God, and pay attention to the answers given. Take responsibility for your decisions and know that your decision matters—not only to you but also to the world and the future.

If you want to partner with God to bless the world, say yes to what God proposes. Start to live with consequences, and go on living with the consequences. There's no shortcut, no easy way, no American-dream-come-true way to partner with God.

But we can do it.

How do I know?

God's maiden did it.

It's the Little Things

Luke 1:39–56

The world is a noisy place filled with larger-than-life people, and if we're not careful, we start to believe that the giants and the noise are the story that matters.

Luke knows better. That's why he gives us the story of Elizabeth and Mary.

Mary goes to the home of Elizabeth. Whether to get some space from her parents and Joseph and her home village or to check out Gabriel's story about Elizabeth, I don't know. Entering the house, she calls out to Elizabeth, and the baby growing in Elizabeth's womb leaps. Elizabeth is filled with the Holy Spirit, discerns Mary's pregnancy and role in God's redemption, and blesses Mary—who probably felt the need to be blessed by a flesh-and-blood person at this point in time.

Mary responds with a poem that we call The Magnificat. And she stays three months with Elizabeth before returning to deal with her family and Joseph.

At first glance, we might think, "Lovely story. Shows a nice connection between Elizabeth and Mary. Glad Luke included it. Time now to move on to bigger things."

Slow down. Luke tells the story for many reasons, not the least of which is to remind us to look for God in the little tales of quiet folk.

So what's God doing here?

To start with, God is working in partnership with women to reshape the world. There's not one man in the story. Keep in mind that the mindset of first-century Judaism and of the first century in general assumed men were the movers and shakers in history. Here, though, we find Mary and Elizabeth doing all the action. There's not a man in sight to supervise them, act in their place, or pass judgment on them or their theological conclusions.

The two women—whom culture tries to keep on the outside looking in—are now insiders. They know what God is doing. The women are partnering with God as the Incarnation starts to find traction in history.

Remember this should you find yourself wondering if a woman can be the first to receive a word from God, take initiative in church leadership, or fulfill a role in the life of the church. God partnered with two women to launch the Incarnation story, and did so without consulting men, without regard for long-established traditions of biblical interpretation, or without attention to cultural norms.

Second, God is working in partnership with the prepared. Elizabeth and Mary are well grounded in the stories of their religious tradition. They know the biblical stories, not least the stories of how God worked in the past with women to bring God's will to pass. Certainly, they know the story of Hannah the mother of Samuel and the song she sang. Mary's song (The Magnificat) owes much to Hannah's.

In ancient Israel, the idea that two women might be the ones best prepared to partner with God was deeply subversive. Most people would have expected God to work through a mighty prophet in the model of Elijah or perhaps through a gifted Pharisee, synagogue leader, or even a Sadducee. If God was about to change the world, surely God could be expected to go to those certified (in one way or another) to lead the people of God.

What makes the preparation of Elizabeth and Mary different? After all, the stories they know are the same stories known to others.

I can't prove it, but I think the difference is that Elizabeth and Mary took the stories to heart and expected God to go on writing new stories in the same vein. I think they recognized God was not finished with God's work and so they were open to God writing a new chapter and sweeping them into the narrative.

We do well to remember that preparation includes two elements. The first, and the one with which we are most comfortable, is knowledge. We learn the stories, sayings, and teachings of the Scripture and how they have been interpreted and applied. The second element is a bit more challenging: we learn to see ourselves in the stories and to live as if we're living within them at all times.

That's why Mary can conceive Jesus and sing The Magnificat. Despite her culture's prejudices, she sees herself as a participant in a story much larger than herself. Well prepared, she sings her worship of the Lord and Savior. She celebrates God's decision to advance God's work through the lowly. With the arsenal of words and concepts at her disposal, she sings of how God's mighty work brings low the mighty and fills the hungry with good things. She sings of the promises of God and of the God who never forgets a promise.

Sometimes I go looking to try to see where God is at work today in the life of the world and the church.

Here's what I've found to be true.

On occasion I might find God at work in the life of a great church council, a revival meeting, a retreat setting, a Bible study group, or even Sunday morning worship. I've even discerned God at work in a business environment or a government office. God can and does show up everywhere.

Most often, though, I've found God working underground, birthing the next breakthrough of God's movement among those overlooked by the world at large and even the church.

If we want to find where God is at work today, we must go look among women, the poor, those in the Third World, the sick, and the exiled.

There's a new story brewing out there among the marginalized, the next chapter in the greater story of God's steadfast love for the world and all who dwell in it.

Count on it.

5

Zechariah's Finest Hour

Luke 1:57–80

Long ago, a church I served as pastor faced a major decision: would we join other congregations and synagogues to provide temporary housing for homeless people from among the working poor?

The discussions surfaced latent racism among some church members, including one particular man. Normally the most welcoming of persons, he found himself afraid to bring "those people" into the church facility. He voiced his concerns in several gatherings and appeared ready to lead an effort to defeat the proposal.

When the day came for the congregation to vote, he rose to speak. What he said surprised everyone.

"As many of you know, I have been against this proposal. I'm ashamed to say I let my fear guide me. I'm sorry. I had not even prayed about the proposal. Finally, I decided I ought to pray about the matter before I voted against the motion. When I prayed, it was as if God spoke to me and said, 'Stop being afraid. You know this is the kind of ministry I want you to support.' So I'm here tonight to urge us to approve the motion, and I want to be among the first to sign up to help."

As you might imagine, the motion passed handily.

When we talked later, I thanked him for his willingness to listen to and trust God, even at the risk of being put in conflict with some of his best friends. I told him I thought his short speech at the business meeting might have been his finest hour.

He blinked back tears and said, "Perhaps. I only wish I might have had such a moment earlier in my life."

None of us live lives filled with an unbroken string of finest moments. All of us, though, may experience a few. Such was the case for Zechariah on the day of his son's birth.

Zechariah's response to Gabriel had not been his finest moment! As a result, he found himself mute from the day of Gabriel's appearance until the birth of John. I suspect he did a great deal of thinking in the time between the two events. On the day John was born, Zechariah rose to the occasion.

Imagine the scene. Elizabeth gives birth to John. As is customary, family members and even some neighbors gather to celebrate, help out, and—as becomes clear—offer unsolicited advice. Perhaps they think Elizabeth and Zechariah are too old and frail to manage matters well. In any case, the family and neighbors try to take charge to ensure everything is handled properly and in accordance with tradition.

Matters come to a head on the eighth day after the birth. According to custom, it is time to name the baby. The family and friends assume he will be named after his father, but Elizabeth shocks the group when she declares the baby will be named John.

The group disputes her choice, and they are on solid ground with regard to tradition and practice. Everyone knows it is traditional to use an established family name. They turn to Zechariah. Surely he will agree with them.

Zechariah rises to the demands of the situation and has his finest hour. He takes a tablet and writes on it that the child's name is John.

Luke tells us the family was "amazed," a term he likes to use to describe how people react to God's work in their midst (v. 63). Perhaps that's the case here, but I think it more likely that the family simply could not imagine a world in which their decision made sense. I can almost hear some of them thinking, "Oh, dear. What are we going to do? Both Zechariah and Elizabeth have lost it. The poor child is going to be stuck with a poorly chosen name!"

The family and friends, with the best of intentions, could not see that their efforts to control the naming ran counter to God's intentions. Who knows what might have happened if they had succeeded? Perhaps the renamed child's life direction would have been reset so that it fell into the familiar patterns of first-century Jewish life.

Zechariah was not finished. His voice restored, he was able to tell the full backstory to John's birth. And, filled with the Spirit, he spoke a prophecy, a true saying, about God and the child.

He declared the God of Israel was to be trusted under all circumstances. As for the baby John, Zechariah declared he would grow to become the prophet who prepared the way for the coming Son of David. John, at his best, would lay the groundwork for the Messiah's ministry of salvation, forgiveness, mercy, and light. Though John would not be the Messiah, his work would pave the road on which the Messiah walked into the lives of the people.

The story of Zechariah's finest hour pushes me to take a hard look at myself. Have there been times when I've tried to squeeze God's dreams and plans into the box of my established expectations of life? Might I be trying to do so even now?

Can I recall times when someone called my hand or did what was needed—in spite of me, or without my help—to advance God's agenda? Do I need someone to do so now?

Perhaps most important, is now the time in the life of my church, family, or circle of friends when I am called to rise to the occasion and have my finest hour?

I know this much: there comes a time in each of our lives when we are called to play the role of Zechariah at his best.

Let's not miss the moment!

6

The Multiple Miracles of Christmas

Luke 2:1-20

"It's a miracle," we say, perhaps a bit too glibly. Yet the hope that drives us to look for miracles is well rooted in our faith, the foundation of which includes the miracle of the Incarnation, that deep mystery of the Word becoming flesh and dwelling among us.

Bound up in that miracle is a collection of smaller—but quite real—miracles. Let's consider the multiple miracles of Christmas.

The First Miracle: Christ was born in the midst of "bad times." I recall the words of a man who was asked what he expected of Christmas. He replied, "Well, I don't know how the spirit of the season will be this year. Times are tough. A dollar doesn't go very far anymore."

Implicit in his comment is the conviction that the tenor of the times determines the possibility of Christmas. He seems to believe bad times might preclude Christmas.

Thank God, such is not the case. Nothing can stop the real Christmas, the coming of the Christ Child.

Consider the state of the world into which Jesus was born. Rome ruled the region, including the homeland of Jesus' parents. King Herod ruled his little corner of the Roman world. Herod brooked no real or imagined rivals.

Illness and early death were the norm, especially among children.

Jesus' family circumstances included tensions with the parents of Mary and Joseph, the social stigma of Mary's pregnancy, and the challenge of making a living in a stagnant economy. Even as the time of Jesus' birth approached, Joseph and Mary were forced to take an unexpected trip to Bethlehem so that Rome could tax them more efficiently.

The times were bad in ways and to a degree that few if any of us can imagine.

But the Word became flesh anyway. The Incarnation happened in the midst of bad times.

Mark it down: bad times cannot stop God's arrival in God's world. Christmas is God's promise that nothing, neither a bad economy, the threat or actuality of war, relationship conundrums, grief, nor anything else can prevent God coming to us.

The Second Miracle: Christ was born to humble and flawed parents. If the religious leaders of the day noticed Mary and Joseph, they probably thought of them as second-class citizens, not least because they lived in Galilee. Conquered only a century or so before the time of Christ, many of the area's inhabitants had been forced to become Jews, and the resulting population was held in low esteem by the people of Judea and Jerusalem.

But Mary and Joseph, while quite worthy of our respect, no doubt struggled to believe what God was doing in their lives. I suspect both entertained a strong distaste or even hatred for Romans.

Their humility was their strength. Both tried to accept and live into the will of God. They were humble, flawed, and disregarded by many, but the Incarnation happened anyway. Jesus was born to them.

And that's good news for us. God does not wait for any of us to get our act together or be taken seriously by others. Instead, God comes anyway.

The Third Miracle: Christ comes for all. Quite contrary to the expectations of many of God's people in the first century, Christ came for all people.

I suspect most first-century Israelites would have argued that the Messiah would come only for the redemption of the Jews. Some, such as the Essenes, might have insisted the Messiah would come only for their particular sect within Judaism.

Christ instead came as good news for all peoples. By the time his story is told fully, we find Jesus is good news for . . .

. . . the shepherds, whom most regard as unclean.

. . . wise Gentiles from the East.

. . . traitors such as Zacchaeus.

. . . Pharisees such as Nicodemus.

. . . fisher folk such as Peter.

. . . women of all sorts such as Mary, Martha, and others.

Sometimes I think we find this the most disconcerting of all the miracles of Christ. Yet it remains true: the Savior has come for the sake of all.

The Fourth Miracle: Christ came at all. Why would the Word become flesh and dwell among us? Why would God make God's home in a world such as this one?

Why bother? Surely that's the question we would ask if we considered whether to come to the rescue of a world in which...

. . . God's people are stuck in a tiresome cycle of sin, consequences for sin, repentance, restoration, and subsequent return to sin.

. . . idolatry is the norm, coupled with cruelty to the poor, sick, conquered, and defenseless.

. . . corruption is commonplace in religion and politics.

Why bother with such a world?

Yet the Word became flesh, God came to us, and God still comes to us. Why?

Because of love that refuses to abandon the world or us.

The greatest of the multiple miracles of Christmas is that God loves the world as it is, and loves it so much that God chooses to enter the world's story and rewrite it from the inside out.

7

Temple Stories

Luke 2:21-52

Start with the stories of Jesus and go where they take you. Lay aside ideologies, assumptions, theologies, and all the other mental constructs that hem us in, and pay attention to the stories as told.

Take, for instance, the two stories Luke tells about Jesus' childhood visits to the temple. They remind us that Jesus cannot be confined even within our most cherished traditions and assumptions.

The first story takes place forty or so days after the birth of Jesus. By tradition, the family goes to offer their firstborn male child to the Lord by making a sacrifice at the temple. The second story takes place when Jesus is twelve years old. Breaking away from the daily routine, Joseph and Mary take Jesus (and the rest of the family) to Jerusalem for Passover.

There's nothing novel about what they do. In fact, they do what any pious first-century Jewish person in the region would do.

Surprising things may happen as we engage in the seemingly mundane actions of the faith. These stories remind us this is so.

Enter Simeon and Anna. Both are old in a culture that equates age with the potential for wisdom. They frequent the temple. Simeon does so for three reasons: he is pious, focused on watching for the arrival of "the consolation of Israel" (v. 25), and led by Holy Spirit. Anna spends all her time at the temple. She is a long-term widow, one of that society's powerless persons. Luke, though, calls her a prophet, someone inspired by God to speak on behalf of God to a given time, context, or situation.

The two take the Holy Family by surprise. Simeon holds Jesus, praises God, declares he now has seen the Lord's Messiah, and announces his readiness to die. He blesses the child. His blessing, though, cannot be said to be comforting. Simeon declares that the child will spark mixed reactions. Some will rise up under his teaching and leadership, while others will choose to oppose him, and Mary will feel as if her very soul has been pierced by a sword before all is resolved.

Anna steps up to the family, praises God, and begins to tell all who will listen that the promised Messiah has come. Mary and Joseph find themselves and the child on public display. I doubt they feel at all comfortable.

Nearly twelve years later, at the end of their trip to Jerusalem to celebrate Passover, Mary and Joseph leave to return home. Later that day, they get to hunting in their traveling group and discover Jesus is not with them. Hastening back to the city, and no doubt fearing the worst, they search for their son for three days. They finally locate him, sitting among the teachers (sitting, as a teacher would sit), listening to them and asking questions. The teachers find him more than able to hold his own in the conversation.

Mary and Joseph are astonished, but Mary is also a worried and irritated parent. She asks, "Child, why have you treated us like this?" Note the use of the term "child." While the teachers have treated Jesus as young adult, Mary speaks of him as a child.

And Jesus answers, "Why were you searching for me? Did you not know that I must be in my Father's house?" (v. 49). Luke tells us neither Mary or Joseph understood his meaning, but I suspect his words reminded them of something they may have wanted to forget: their child was God's Son, and he would one day take up God's work rather than live the normal life of a firstborn son.

When I pay serious attention to the surprises in the two temple stories, I get a little nervous. Is it possible that God continues to slip surprises into our religious routines—revelations small and large?

Yes. For example, one of my religious routines is to read the annual edition of *The Best American Spiritual Writing*. An essay written by Robert Coles caught my attention. He wrote about an experience with his fifth-grade teacher. One day, she moved outside the routine, stepped away from math and reading, and said the following words to the class: "We are entitled to travel on our own paths, but here and now we are walking together . . . . We should pay attention to others as well as ourselves . . . . We spend time looking at ourselves and looking out for ourselves, but please, let us look to our right and to our left, to our front and to what's going on to our back. Please be mindful of others, as we hope they will be of us."[1]

There in the middle of one of my routine religious observances, God poked me in the chest and gave me words to describe the challenge of living the Golden Rule in a society given to runaway individualism.

Think back, search your memory, and you will recall occasions when God spoke to you in the midst of reading Scripture, praying, singing a hymn, hearing a sermon, listening to another, or engaging in some other faith practice. Chances are, each such occasion heightened your sense of living in God's world as one of God's children, of being caught up in a story larger than yourself, of being someone reshaped into the image of God not only for your own sake but for the sake of God's work in the world.

It turns out that God uses even the routine practices of the faith to shake us up.

Throw yourself into the practices and disciplines of the faith. At the very least, they will help shape your mind and heart. God may also drop in a surprise that rattles you at your core and opens your eyes to see new possibilities.

Note

1. Robert Coles, "Here and Now We Are Walking Together," *The Best American Spiritual Writing, 2004* (New York: Houghton Mifflin Company, 2004) 29.

8

Preparing for Jesus

Luke 3:1-20

For some time now, I've been trying to listen to Luke 3:1-20, and the longer I do so the more it speaks to me of preparation for Christmas. Merchants know a great deal about such preparation. I saw my first advertisement for Christmas in early September. Based on what I hear in the hallways and see on Facebook, some of us are masters of Christmas preparation. Even a quick glance at the church calendar makes it clear we are devoted to preparing for Christmas.

The story of John the Baptist calls us to focus on preparing for Jesus to arrive in the world and in our hearts.

The longer I live with the text, the more I realize God had been preparing for Jesus for a very long time. I love the particulars in the opening verses: dates, names of various rulers and two high priests, and locations. It's as if God looked at God's calendar and said, "The perfect time has come at last!"

In Luke's time, writers would often make a list of the high and mighty and follow the list with stories of what these individuals had done. Luke, though, surprises his readers, not with a story of the mighty, but of the lowly: "the word of God came to John son of Zechariah in the wilderness" (v. 2). It is as if Luke is saying that while the eyes of the world focus on the doings of the powerful, God moves among the common.

There's irony here. God started down the long road toward the coming of Jesus from the moment our kind went astray. Eventually God called out a people, and their prophets—such as Isaiah, Jeremiah, and a host of others—told God's people to pray and live toward the day when God would bring the work to fruition.

Yet, when the time finally comes in our text, almost no one is watching. Their attention is elsewhere, drawn to and captured by the great affairs of the empire or at least by what is happening in their little piece of it.

Advent, if we allow it, draws our eyes away from the great matters of the world and refocuses them on the current presence and work of Christ. The promise of Advent is that if we look among the poor, weak, oppressed, and humble, we will see Christ in them and the work Christ is doing.

The longer I live with the text, the more I realize I can prepare the way for Jesus to enter and take up residence in me. Advent preparation is about more than seeing Jesus; it calls us to clear the way for Jesus to make his home with us.

John drew a crowd to the Jordan River. He preached and taught how each person might prepare for the coming of the Lord, how each might make straight the paths, level the valleys and mountains, and smooth the way for the Lord to come, stay, and rule in their lives.

"Teacher, what should we do?" they asked (v. 12). Soldiers, tax collectors, everyday people—in fact, almost every kind of person other than political and religious leaders asked the question. John gave specific answers, replies apt to the particular life situation of each questioner.

To the soldier he said, "Stop shaking down people for bribes and start living on your wages. Do the work of soldiers: protect people." To the everyday folk, the working folk who were just trying to get by, he said, "Whoever has two coats must share with anyone who has none; and whoever has food must do likewise." To the tax collectors, who worked on commission, he said, "Collect only what is due and no more."

In short, John told them to repent. But his kind of repentance bore little resemblance to the generalized, emotion-driven, "I'm sorry, Lord" repentance we often practice. John's kind of repentance interfaced with the core orientation and activities of people's lives. He told them to start treating others as they would wish others to treat them. Interesting, isn't it, that John tied repentance to community-building matters such as sharing life's basic necessities, honesty, and integrity.

Try this. Imagine you're there by the Jordan River listening to John declare that the promised Messiah is coming, and you call out, "What should I do?"

What answer do you think John might give you?

When you find the answer and act on it, you smooth the road into your heart; you ease the way for Jesus to enter and take up residence in your life.

The longer I live with the text, the more I realize we prepare the way for Jesus by taking our proper place in relation to Jesus. Some in the crowd gathered at the river pressured John to declare himself the promised one, the Messiah. John declined to do so. Instead, he placed himself under the authority of the one yet to come. He said, "but one who is more powerful than I is coming; I am not worthy to untie the thong of his sandals" (v. 16).

With those words, John showed the folk of his time and us how to prepare for Jesus. He took his proper place in relation to Jesus, the place of a servant.

John got it right. Let's follow his lead.

The longer I live with the text, the more I realize we prepare for Jesus by choosing to live with the consequences of serving Jesus. Face it: John's life did not play out happily. He spoke truth to power (in his case, to Herod). As a result, Herod imprisoned him and later took his life. John accepted the consequences of serving the promised Messiah.

Therein lay John's power to make a difference for God in the world as the world is: he took his proper place in God's scheme of things, stayed true to the vision God provided, and accepted the consequences. In doing so, he paved the way for Jesus.

A saying has made the rounds the past few years: "Elections have consequences." Advent preparation does, too. If we get in touch with what God is doing in the world, smooth the way of Jesus into our hearts by genuine repentance, and start to live into the changes wrought by repentance, there will be consequences.

We will worship more often and fully, redirect our resources and skills to godly ends, speak up for others and become good neighbors to all, and rile those who would prefer the world remain unchanged. As a consequence, our lives may become more complicated and less easy, yet they may also become the kinds of lives that bring the gospel to bear in all the venues of life.

I don't think it's easy to take up or continue in such a life. John certainly found it challenging. I've found it useful to pray the following prayer on a regular basis, and I offer it now to you.

Lord, help us prepare for Jesus so that he may come without delay to us, enter into us, and dwell there from this day forward.

Teach us the possibilities and costs of genuine repentance, and grant us wisdom enough to see and deal with those aspects of our lives that might hinder the entry or reign of Jesus.

Strengthen our courage that we might live into our repentance and into the new life Jesus gives. Help us accept whatever consequences may follow.

This is our prayer, offered in the name of the Christ. Amen.

9

The Temptations

Luke 3:21–4:13

At Jesus' baptism, God spoke and affirmed something I suspect Mary had told Jesus many times: "You are my Son, the Beloved; with you I am well pleased" (v. 21). Jesus took the words to heart. Insofar as I can tell, he lived the rest of his life with a clear sense of his identity.

Knowing who and what he was, Jesus undertook a necessary and difficult task. He withdrew into the wilderness to fast and pray so that he could discern how best to be the Son of God in the world. Luke tells us he spent forty days wrestling with the question, rejecting a variety of options, and settling on the core approach he would follow even if doing so led to the cross. Jesus considered and rejected three options or temptations.

The first might be labeled *the economic option*. Jesus lived in a world familiar with poverty and famine. Genuine hunger threatened the majority of the population at any given time. Many people made their living as day laborers who earned just about enough to purchase a day's supply of bread.

How might the Son of God get the attention of most people in that time, convince them of his power, and enlist them as followers? Provide them with bread. Feed them. Meet their most immediate and recurring need. Keep doing so, even as Moses was said to have provided daily manna in the wilderness.

Jesus rejected the option. Mind you, he did not reject the need to feed the hungry! Instead, he insisted that humans cannot be made whole by bread alone. We need food, but we need more than food to thrive. What we need will be revealed through the words and deeds of Jesus as Luke's Gospel unfolds.

The second temptation might be labeled *the way of coercive power*. Jesus was shown all the kingdoms of the world, and the tempter declared all this would be given to Jesus if only Jesus agreed to worship him.

Win the world by getting, keeping, and exercising political and military power—that's the essence of the temptation. The tempter's argument went something like this: "If you want to change the world, take over the world. That's how Rome is changing the world. Sure, blood gets spilt, but look at the benefits: secure borders, a shared economy, better and safer roads, a common language for law and commerce. Look at the Romans: they don't hesitate to take power and use it. You're the Son of God. Surely you have the right to take power and use it. Once you have power, you can reshape the world to suit yourself."

The second temptation is alive and well in our time. Whenever we start to think the world would be a better place if only Christians held the reins of governmental and military power, we're hearing the voice of the tempter.

Jesus rejects the option because he sees its fatal flaw. The way of coercive power requires those who follow it to practice idolatry. Throughout his ministry, Jesus consistently refused to take up the sword even in his own defense, let alone to force others to do his will. Will you and I have wisdom enough to follow Jesus' lead?

The third option might be labeled *playing to the crowd.* As Luke puts it, the tempter took Jesus to the pinnacle of the temple in Jerusalem and told him to throw himself off it so that God might send angels to catch and bear him safely to the ground. The temptation was based on a popular expectation that the Messiah would appear suddenly at the top of the temple. Had Jesus chosen to give in, no doubt many people would have flocked to him. Never mind that doing so would require Jesus to test God.

The temptation of playing to the crowd besets the church, doesn't it? It does so because it promises to deliver followers, finances, and power for those who succumb to it. In the United States, prime examples include pastors, media preachers, and politicians who proclaim the health and wealth gospel or fan the flames of racism or xenophobia.

Remember, Jesus rejected the temptation. Will you and I follow his lead?

The three temptations have something in common: each offered Jesus a relatively safe way to pursue his ministry as the Son of God. If he chose one of the three options—at least according to the tempter—Jesus would avoid suffering and win the day. The only thing he would be required to sacrifice was his trust in God alone.

Jesus opted for unbridled trust in God. May we be given the wisdom and courage to do the same.

10

There's Room at the Canvas

Luke 4:14–30

Do you sometimes find it daunting that God invites you to join in the work God is doing in the world? Are you afraid to start or make a mistake? Perhaps you think God might have mistaken you for someone else, someone more talented, spiritual, or wise?

How do we move past our hesitancy, step up, and get started? I've found a way that works for me (most days!).

Start with an image: God the Master Artist standing before a canvas, creating a painting with the working title, "God's World the Way It Ought to Be."

Imagine God the painter at work. Personally, I picture God dressed in old clothes spattered with various colors of paint. I watch as God selects a brush, dips it in the paints, and carefully adds an element to the emerging painting.

Luke 4:14 and following describe what God is trying to paint: a world in which all kinds of people—including those in the most desperate situations—experience God as love, release, recovery, abundance, and good news.

Get the picture?

Here's how I connect the image to Jesus. Jesus stands in his hometown synagogue and declares that he has come to implement God's vision of the world as it ought to be. He does so in front of folk, God-worshipers all, who think they know him yet are given to being fearful or contemptuous of the kinds of people named in the list from Isaiah, which Jesus cites.

Jesus says God's mission is fulfilled in him, that such work is what God's Messiah has come to do. And Jesus invites God's people to join him in partnering with God on such a mission.

Instead of doing so, they get angry, reject the call, and attempt to kill Jesus. No doubt much to their surprise, they cannot touch him. Jesus goes on his way, lives in accordance with the vision, and calls people to join in the work.

God the artist goes on painting "God's World the Way It Ought to Be." Through Christ, God says to each of us, "Won't you come and paint alongside me?"

I used to think God meant, "Come and paint by the numbers." Surely, I thought, God has already sketched in everything and only wants me to fill in the spaces. Given my history with "paint by the numbers," I found the thought discouraging (I've never been good at painting inside the lines). More seriously, "painting by the numbers" denies the reality of the uniqueness and creativity of each of us, individuals made in the image of the creative God.

However, I eventually realized that God wants me to take a place at the canvas and bring my particular gifts to bear. When I realized God wants me to use my eye for color, design, and shape and call on my life experience, I felt freed to take hold of a brush and start painting. I began to do what I could to work alongside God to paint "God's World the Way It Ought to Be."

The longer I paint, the more I learn that everyday women and men do this all the time. It's how we work with God.

I know a group of older women who knit caps for infants and children who are patients at a local hospital. Their work makes the world a little more the way the world ought to be for such children, their families, and their medical caregivers.

I remember a younger ministerial friend who struggled for years to decide if he could be faithful to God and be a pastor. Finally, he made peace with his actual gifts and put them to work in the congregation he had. The results continue to astound me. His church has become a place in which one hears the words of Jesus, finds unconditional welcome, is freed to stand with the downtrodden, and experiences a fusion of the worlds of religion and music. This happened because my friend stepped up to the canvas and started painting, not by the numbers, but in accordance with his actual gifts and experience. As a result, his little piece of the world looks a little more like "God's World as It Ought to Be."

There's a women's Bible study group in our church whose members are painting alongside God. The group is gifted with some people connected to ministries that bring clean water to the poor of the world. The class couples this connection with their remarkable gifts for sales and organization, and leads the church to raise funds to provide water filters. The class members use the gifts, skills, and relationships they possess to make the world a little more the way it ought to be.

Some of our church members with the gifts of hospitality and love choose to minister to people with HIV in Knoxville. Partnering with a Christian nonprofit and another congregation, they now provide food, transportation to medical appointments, and friendship to people living with the disease. Because of them, the world is a little more the way it ought to be in Knoxville, Tennessee.

Get the picture?

Each day, I try to take up my brush and colors and paint the portion of the canvas I can reach. I try to do this in partnership with God the Master Artist. I do so in hopes that by joining with God and all the others working on the canvas, I might help create the great painting of God's dream, the painting called "God's World the Way It Ought to Be."

There's a place at the canvas for you. Will you take it?

11

A Meditation on Ministry

Luke 4:31–44

In ministry, rejection and success pose challenges. This is true for clergy, laypeople, and congregations. What are we to do when individuals or communities reject or try to stop our ministry? Just as important, what are we to do when people embrace our ministries yet try to lay exclusive claim to our presence and time?

As always, Jesus provides guidance. When the people of his hometown Nazareth rejected him, he went on his way and set up shop in Capernaum, a small city in Galilee, where he continued with his ministry.

He taught as one who had authority, healed many, and set others free of whatever held dominion over their lives. As a result, many flocked to him. His success bred a problem: the people of Capernaum tried to claim him for their own and prevent him from going elsewhere to help others. He refused to be so bound, and once again he went on his way.

Jesus went about his ministry in the way he believed to be faithful to God, regardless of the response of others. As a result, he fulfilled his God-given mission.

I think Christians such as Francis of Assisi, John Woolman, and Martin Luther King, Jr., grasped and followed such a principle. Perhaps that is why each was able to reshape the church and world of their eras.

I wonder what our congregation, you, or I might accomplish through our ministries if only we followed the lead of Jesus the way these individuals did.

Don't you think it's well past time we found out?

12

How Will I Draw Others toward Christ?

Luke 5:1–11

What kinds of feelings stir when you read and consider Luke 5:1-11? How do you feel about our Jesus-assigned responsibility to bring the good news to others?

I suppose it's possible you might respond, "I feel great! I can't think of anything else I would rather do. It comes naturally to me."

Most of us, though, would offer other answers.

"Well, I've really tried."

"I've tried a few times, but I didn't have a good experience."

"I've been turned off by methods and attitudes I've seen in others, so I've backed off."

"To tell the truth, it's been a long time since I've given it much thought."

"I feel rather guilty about the entire matter."

Personally, I've always wanted to become more intentional and better about introducing others to the God I know in Jesus Christ. For years, though, I struggled to find a way other than the slightly baptized but scarcely damp sales techniques found in most action plans. I cannot believe manipulation of any sort has a place in sharing the good news.

There is a better way. We start to discern it when we take Luke 5:1-11 seriously.

Recall the storyline. Jesus is teaching by the shores of the Lake of Gennesaret (Lake of Galilee) when he spots two boats at the shoreline. One belongs to Simon. Jesus climbs into the boat and asks Simon to put out from the shore, after which Jesus continues to teach the gathered crowd.

When Jesus finishes teaching, he says something outlandish to Simon: "Put out into the deep water and let down your nets" (v. 4). Simon, a fisherman by trade, knows better. He and his fellow fishermen have already fished all night (the proper time for fishing on the Lake of Galilee), but they have caught nothing. Now, they've just finished washing their nets. It's time to rest in preparation for another night's work.

Still, solely because it's Jesus asking, Simon does as requested. He and his coworkers let down the nets, which fill with so many fish the nets start to break. They signal to their partners in the other boat to come and help them. Both boats fill with fish and start to flounder in the water.

Simon falls to his knees and begs Jesus to go away from him. He does not feel worthy to be in the presence of Jesus. But Jesus responds, "Do not be afraid; from now on you will be catching people" (v. 10). The fishermen bring the boats to shore, and from that moment Simon, James, and John leave their workplace and home to follow Jesus.

How does the story help us find our way toward becoming better at introducing others to Jesus?

Start by paying close attention to what Jesus said and did. He did not say to the apostles in the making, "I'm calling you because you are naturals at introducing people to God." Nor did he say, "Follow me down to the marketplace, where I know someone who will teach you how to close a sale."

Instead, Jesus tells them not to be afraid. He assures them that they will become people who help others know and follow Jesus. Then Jesus starts walking. All they are called to do in the moment is follow after him and learn from him.

They become his disciples. I think "apprentices" might be a better term to use. "Apprentice" is a useful way to think about discipleship. We are apprenticed to Jesus in order to learn by observation and practice how to live the Jesus life, including how to share the good news of Christ in ways that honor God and respect others.

What does apprenticeship require? I can think of four elements. We make a decision that we want to apprentice ourselves to Jesus. In addition, we treat him as our master. We give the apprenticeship time enough to work, and we move through levels of expertise until we reach our personal maximum level of accomplishment.

Try using "apprentice" as a synonym for "disciple." I think you'll find it works.

When we apprentice ourselves to Jesus, we start to learn a great deal about how best to draw others to God. What did Jesus do? As you find answers, you will start to see how Jesus drew others to God and will learn to imitate his ways.

Five terms capture some of what I have learned along the way with Jesus. I offer them for your consideration.

Mobility. Jesus moved out with God and among people. He stayed on the move, and he encountered and interacted with a wide range of people. His approach differs sharply from our tendency to move mostly in established circles and to connect only with those we already know or like. If you and I are going to get better at sharing the good news, we've got to get out and about and mix with people.

Teaching. Jesus spent most of his time teaching. If we model ourselves on Jesus, we must dare to become learners and to share what we learn. This runs counter to our tendency to settle for what we already know. Teaching remains a crucial aspect of making disciples.

Healing. Jesus practiced a healing ministry among the sick, poor, and outcasts. He brought the good news that God sees and loves such folk, though they lived in a culture that usually excluded and neglected them. Jesus moved among them without fear. In my experience, we all too often cast blame, hope someone else helps, or hold back because of some kind of fear. It's past time we emulated the approach of Jesus.

Sacrificing. Jesus gave up whatever he had to give up in order to become the presence of God to people. He walked away from his trade and surrendered the respect he might have enjoyed as the head of his family. Jesus had no place to lay his head. He suffered abuse of various kinds. In the end, he laid down his life. Apprenticeship requires sacrifice of time, anonymity, established worldviews, self-centeredness, careers, and sometimes life itself.

Inviting. Jesus always called people to see and enter the kingdom of God. A good apprentice does the same. Remember, we're not asking people to join the church or adopt our particular lifestyles. Instead, we are to invite them to go looking for what God is doing in the world and in their lives.

Apprentices learn and in time embrace the methods of Jesus. Some of us will be better than others at any given practice, but the more we live into all of them, the more nearly we will become genuine disciple-makers.

I know. It sounds a bit overwhelming. The truth, though, is that such apprenticeship is doable. It is the way of life to which all of us are called.

When do we start? As it was for the first disciples/apprentices, so it is for us: it's best to start now.

13

Will They Call Us "Friend"?

Luke 5:12–32

Not too long ago, I sat in on an informal gathering of folk concerned about their congregation's declining impact in their town. They had invited me to help them think through the matter, identify possible ways to address it, and settle on recommended actions.

They found it hard to reach a consensus on the causes of the decline, let alone what to do about it. Some lamented changes in the racial, economic, and linguistic make-up of the town. Others focused on the congregation's internal life and maintained that the key to reaching their community lay in changes to worship, the church staff, formation resources, and in facility renovations.

Eventually, the conversation wound down, and they asked me to share my impressions. I reviewed the situation and summarized their conversation, and they agreed I had heard them correctly. Then I asked a question: "How do you think the various people groups and individuals in the town who don't participate in congregational life might describe your congregation?"

Silence ensued. As it turned out, no one had asked that question. I took a chance and suggested some possible positive and negative answers.

I then turned the conversation in a slightly different direction and asked, "How would you hope they perceived you?" The group quickly came up with a long list of possibilities, which we recorded. When finished, we reviewed the list and quickly concluded that we needed to find some way to encompass the best of them in a single statement.

The subsequent conversation took quite some time, but in the end we came up not with a statement but a question: "Will they call us 'Friend?'"

Luke 5:12-32 suggests Jesus would approve of such an approach.

I suspect the leper would have called Jesus, "Friend." Think it through. Lepers lived as outcasts cut off from family, friends, the synagogue, and society. They were forbidden to come near healthy people, let alone share a touch with them. Yet the leper felt able to approach Jesus, and Jesus actually reached out and touched him. Jesus healed him, too. Jesus treated the leper as a friend rather than problem.

Don't you think the friends of the paralytic and the paralytic himself would have called Jesus, "Friend"? I do. Jesus affirmed the faith displayed by the paralytic's friends; in fact, he said their faith played a decisive role in their friend's healing. As for the paralytic himself, he felt new life surge through his limbs as Jesus declared his sins forgiven. When Jesus told him to rise, take his pallet, and walk to his home, he was able to do so. The man heard Jesus dismiss the theological objections some scribes and Pharisees raised, though doing so angered these powerful religious authorities. Jesus allowed no arguments to get in the way of helping the man. He treated him as a friend rather than problem.

Levi the tax collector certainly would have come to call Jesus, "Friend." Think about Levi's situation. He collected taxes for the Roman oppressors. As a result, most of his fellow Jews shunned him as a traitor. Many tax collectors overcharged and pocketed the difference. We don't know if Levi did so, but no doubt most people assumed he did. The revolutionary sect called the Zealots may well have had him on their list of persons to be assassinated. Aside from fellow tax collectors and a handful of others, Levi had few friends.

Then one day, as Levi sat in the tax collector's booth, Jesus stopped by and said to him, "Follow me." Mind you, Levi would have heard about Jesus. People were talking about the healing miracles, teachings, and those Jesus had called to follow him. I doubt, though, that Levi had ever imagined that Jesus might figure into his own life. Now, out of the blue, Jesus enters his life not as a judge or enemy but instead with an invitation. Levi responded by inviting Jesus into the sanctuary of his own home to meet more people like Levi.

Some Pharisees and scribes complained yet again: "Why do you eat and drink with tax collectors and sinners?" (v. 30). We sometimes miss the sincerity of their question. Table fellowship mattered in those days. It implied acceptance of those with whom one shared the meal. The Pharisees and scribes deeply believed that Jesus offended God by eating and drinking with tax collectors and sinners. Jesus, however, insisted he was doing God's will. He treated Levi and the others as friends rather than problems.

The next time we catch ourselves thinking of people as problems to be solved, let's remember and embrace Jesus' approach to people. Who are the marginalized, neglected, and judged of our time? Are we treating them as theological, social, or political problems or instead as individuals to befriend?

How do such folk perceive us? I find it helps to personalize the matter. Sometimes I imagine myself standing before Jesus when all is said and done. Much to my surprise, I see a host of others standing behind me and to my side, and Jesus says to them, "How did you perceive him?" My hope, birthed and nurtured in what I know of Jesus, is that they answer, "We call him 'Friend.'"

14

A Meditation: Round Pegs in Square Holes

Luke 5:33–6:11

"You can't put round pegs in square holes," goes an old saying. We hear it, nod our heads, and say, "That's right. Anyone can see that's true. Who in the world would try to pound round pegs into square holes?"

Strange to tell, religious people often try to do so. One of my great-aunts comes to mind. A faithful member of a small Presbyterian church and well acquainted with large portions of the Bible, she thought she understood how life was supposed to work under God. Unfortunately—and like most of us—she did not get everything right.

For example, interracial marriage confused her. Try as she might, she could not fit it into her worldview. The more we talked, the better I understood she was trying to fit a round peg into a square hole. Her assumptions about biblical teaching and white supremacy made her unable to imagine a world in which people of different races might wed with God's blessing.

I don't think she ever seriously entertained the possibility of discarding her perspective in favor of another one capable of accommodating this new thing (new, at least, to her) that God was doing. To do so would have required her to reshape her very religion.

Knowing her, I better understand the Pharisees who complained when Jesus' disciples did not fast as they thought proper but instead ate and drank with enthusiasm. I can comprehend their attachment to a view of the Sabbath that made Sabbath observance more important than meeting human need.

When I remember my aunt, I can imagine why some Pharisees grew so angry that they began to plot against Jesus. My aunt believed sincerely that interracial marriage offended God. She was wrong, but she believed she was defending the honor of God. It's amazing how angry we become when we think we're standing up for God.

Jesus' words about new wine moved neither the Pharisees nor my aunt. Both knew and preferred the taste of the wine they already had in hand.

Let's go back to the image of square pegs and round holes. I wonder, how many of us are busy trying to force square pegs into round holes? How many of us keep trying to force God's love to fit into the worldview we already hold?

Think on such things as you pray the following prayer:

> Lord Jesus, we confess that we are attached to the way we view the world and the Scriptures. Help us, lest we hide ourselves from what you are doing in the church and the world. Save us from becoming bewildered or angered by what you are doing. Lead us instead to lay aside all we think we know in favor of what you have to show us. Such is our prayer. Amen.

15

Luke's Take on the Beatitudes

Luke 6:12–26

Each Gospel writer interprets Jesus. Keep that in mind as you read the four canonical Gospels.

The contrast between Luke and Matthew's accounts of the Beatitudes illustrates the matter. I'm not particularly concerned with whether Jesus spoke from a mountainside or a level place near the mountain, but I start to pay attention when Matthew writes, "Blessed are the poor in spirit," while Luke writes, "Blessed are the poor" (Mt 5:3; Lk 6:20, version mine).

If we take the Scriptures seriously, what are we to make of such variations? We might try to harmonize the two accounts, I suppose, but I think it's better to accept the differences and deal with where they take us.

Luke's version of the Beatitudes is more radical than Matthew's. In fact, Luke's account fits rather neatly with Jesus' contention that the kingdom of God inverts the structures and values of the world as we know it.

I don't know any way to soften the matter. In Luke, Jesus tells his disciples to look for blessing where no one in all the world finds it: in poverty, hunger, weeping, persecution, and the like. Jesus goes on to warn that what most consider a blessing may turn out to be a curse: financial security, full bellies, mirth, and social acceptance.

Let's add to the quandary. In Jesus' day, most Jewish people probably thought riches, ample food, and a good reputation were signs of God's favor, proof that one was righteous in the eyes of God. Conversely, most believed poverty, want, and social stigma were signs of God's punishment for sin, whether that person's sin or the sin of someone else in their family.

Let's be clear: the words of Jesus ran counter to the majority religious opinion of the day.

If you and I buy into all this, where might it take us? It seems to me that Matthew chose to spiritualize the sayings. What he has Jesus say is certainly true, but his language tones down the rawness of Jesus' reversal of our normal suppositions. Most of us, for example, have little problem believing the "poor in spirit" are blessed of God. Surely God blesses the humble! But we stagger more than a bit when we try to bring together "blessed are the poor" with our hopes, dreams, and practices regarding wealth.

What are we to do? I suggest we start by looking for the potential blessing in each state described by Jesus.

Where's the potential blessing in poverty, hunger, and being despised by some because you align yourself with Christ?

That's where Miss Sadie comes into the story.

Miss Sadie lived in a small town in the Deep South of the United States. She was white, and in those days that mattered to lots of people. Miss Sadie had never married. She lived on a small Social Security check, had no medical insurance of any kind in the pre-Medicare era, and suffered from a number of chronic illnesses.

The little metal trailer in which she lived boasted a bedroom, a tiny bathroom, a hot plate, a refrigerator, and a living room. A freestanding electric heater provided meager warmth in the winter. The trailer had no air-conditioning of any kind, and it was a cruel place to live in the midst of a Southern summer.

Miss Sadie owned a small electric fan. She had discovered it at the city dump one day, brought it home, plugged it in, and found—to her delight—that it ran. She called the fan her "little blessing from God."

Miss Sadie was a Christian, a Methodist by background but, by temperament, more of an independent follower of Jesus.

She was old and had no living family insofar as anyone knew, and frankly no one in the community quite knew what to do with her.

I suppose they might have tried a little harder to help her, except she had what they considered "funny" notions about black people, in particular about the black people who lived in the other trailers in the trailer park.

She spoke of them as her friends, sometimes had one or more of them come over to share small meals in her trailer, occasionally visited their church (the black Baptist church in town, to be precise), and even once hobbled down to the county courthouse to try to help one of her black friends register to vote.

"Poor, old Miss Sadie"—at least that's what the gentler white people in the town said. Others used stronger language as they denigrated her.

Here's the thing: Miss Sadie had no money, health insurance, or anything else most of us think is crucial to the good life. Because of her poverty and her treatment of her black neighbors, she did not enjoy the esteem of the folks who ran things. When she was sick, she suffered without medical care. And when she died, she passed alone in the middle of a hot August night and was buried in a pauper's grave.

When I read, "Blessed are you who are poor, for yours is the kingdom of God. Blessed are you who are hungry now, for you will be filled. Blessed are you who weep now, for you will laugh. Blessed are you when people hate you, and when they exclude you, revile you, and defame you on account of the Son of Man," I think of Miss Sadie (vv. 20-22).

And I catch a glimpse of the potential blessing inherent in poverty, hunger, and being excluded from the dominant society. What's the potential blessing? In a word, freedom. When we've got nothing, we have nothing to lose. Strangely enough, if we choose to exercise it, we have the freedom to practice reliance on God, contentment in all things, and love toward all others.

"Impossible to believe," we snort, and turn away to go on about life as we've known it.

Perhaps. All I can say in return is, "Jesus thought it was possible, and Miss Sadie proved it so."

16

Love and Judgment

Luke 6:27-49

Will we hear Jesus as he speaks a God-grounded, reasonable word about love?

Jesus starts by acknowledging the way we usually perceive and practice love: love those who love you and love only the trustworthy. Such limits on love seem wise, yet they lead to a world that functions on the basis of an eye for an eye and a tooth for a tooth. Love limited in such a way fractures humans into clans and sanctifies conflict. I suppose such limited love is better than no love at all, but it falls short of God's kind of love.

Jesus calls us to a broader, deeper kind of love. "Love your actual enemies and those who despise you," he says.

Those who heard his words in the days of his life had a ready list of enemies: Romans, Samaritans, and in some cases even first-century Jews who belonged to a sub-group of Judaism other than their own.

Be honest. Isn't it easy to list those you regard as enemies? I once asked a rather fearful person to tell me her list of enemies. She was not the sort of person to hold back. In the space of a couple of minutes, she rattled off quite a list, complete with commentary: terrorists, liberal Democrats, her sister and all her sister's friends, a colleague at work, her deceased mother, black people, Communists, and so-called Christians who had "deceived" her daughter and led her to join a mainstream church.

When I asked her about Jesus' command to love our enemies, she looked me in the eye and said, "Jesus did not know the kind of people on my list." She meant it.

Jesus meant what he said, too. I wonder what difference following his command might make in our daily speech, attitudes, and politics. Can we start to imagine the potential impact in a church, family system, circle of acquaintances, city, or the world at large?

Jesus calls us to embrace and practice God's kind of love, which is always sacrificial, costly, and—frankly—derided by many.

What does such love look like in practice? It looks a lot like what we see Jesus doing: interaction, conversation, prayer, teaching, ministering, and always being willing to suffer and die for the sake of others, if need be.

Will we hear Jesus as he speaks a God-grounded, reasonable word about judging others?

Jesus acknowledges the way we normally practice judging others. We assume we have the right, responsibility, and wisdom to pass judgment. We're mistaken.

We're much like a little girl I watched at a beach one day, who spent the morning passing judgment on her little brother's sandcastle. She made it clear that he had built it wrong, mostly because he had not built it as she thought he should have. She told him he did not know how to use his bucket and shovel. Then she kicked down his castle and started to build what she thought he ought to have built. About that time, a wave rushed in and washed away her work. Her so-called wisdom didn't amount to much in the face of the power and reality of the ocean.

Maybe if she had practiced a little humility and grace, both of them could have enjoyed building something before the tide rose and the waves arrived.

I try not to listen to political and religious radio broadcasts, but when I do I usually find someone passing judgment on entire groups of people. As far as I can tell, the only result is to add to the pain and fragmentation of the church and the world.

Presuming to have the wisdom and the right to pass judgment on others is not a reasonable way to live. Jesus calls us to surrender such a way of life in favor of his way. He calls us to remove the log from our own eyes—to face our own prejudices, develop humility, and start to grow into people who practice mercy toward all (v. 42).

Jesus promises that if we do so, we may grow into people who can help others see, find, and remove the speck from their eyes (v. 41).

Jesus lived his life as a reasonable person in an incomprehensible world. I think he found it to be a lonely life. He offers us the opportunity to enter into a new kind of life characterized by the order God intends for God's world.

Some have always listened to, accepted, and embodied the dream of Jesus. They have often been the lonely but godly voices of order and reason in a world given to hate and fear-driven chaos.

It's time, past time, for us to join their ranks.

17

A Meditation: Christ Is with Us

Luke 7

The longer I live with the four stories found in Luke 7, the more I find they speak to me of the Christ who is always with us regardless of external or personal circumstances.

The centurion, a widow, John the Baptist, a sinful woman, and even the Pharisee who judges both her and Jesus—Jesus deals with each of them where he finds them.

Start with the centurion. Though friendly to Judaism, perhaps even a God fearer, he is a Gentile and Roman. He lives in a world defined by power, duty, and authority. I suspect he is more than a little superstitious (Roman soldiers were notorious in this regard).

When the synagogue leaders find Jesus and urge him to come and heal the centurion's slave, Jesus does not hesitate. He does not investigate the centurion's theology or probe the synagogue leadership's claim that the man is worthy. He simply starts toward the centurion's house. When all is said and done, the centurion's servant is healed, and Jesus marvels at the faith of this soldier of Rome.

Jesus is willing to go to the centurion and meet him on his own ground without imposing prior conditions. Perhaps that's a small miracle hidden within the larger miracle story.

Next comes the widow in Nain, who has lost her only son to death. She is shrouded in loss and entirely focused on the funeral procession and pending burial of her son. I doubt she even notices Jesus' arrival. She certainly makes no request of Jesus. Yet he intervenes, restores her son to life, and gives her (not to mention her son) renewed hope.

Then there's John the Baptist, the prophet who foretold the coming of Christ and helped launch the public ministry of Jesus. Neither life in general nor Jesus in particular has met John's expectations. In fact, as far as John can discern from his prison, Jesus might not even be the Messiah. The fearless prophet is now afraid that he was mistaken about Jesus and he's not above threatening to withdraw his support of Jesus.

Jesus does not scold John but instead reminds him of the mission of the Messiah as described by Isaiah. "Tell John," says Jesus, "to look at what I'm doing and to see that it fulfills Isaiah's vision of the Messiah." No one knows how John reacted to the message, but this I do know: Jesus met John where John was, at the point of his doubt and despair.

Finally, Luke tells us about the day Simon the Pharisee invites Jesus to dinner. Simon does so in order to size up Jesus. He wants to decide for himself if Jesus is a righteous person, perhaps even a prophet. To put it another way, Simon presumes himself capable of judging Jesus.

A woman known to be a sinner enters the home and begins to weep at Jesus' feet. She anoints them with expensive ointment, dries them with her hair, and kisses them.

The woman and Simon think themselves quite different from one another. Simon sees himself as righteous, able to judge both Jesus and the woman, and perhaps even responsible to do so. The woman sees herself as a sinner whose only hope lies in God's forgiveness.

Jesus meets both of them where they are in the moment. He deals gently with the woman and gives her the one thing she most needs: assurance of forgiveness. Jesus also gives Simon what he most needs: a sharp reminder of Simon's own need for forgiveness.

We do not know what either Simon or the woman did afterwards. What I do know is that Jesus met both of them where they were.

Jesus does the same with us. When I look out over a congregation, I see people who in that moment are living in a wide variety of places. Some are smug. Others are filled with doubt. Many are dealing with some kind of loss. A few are filled with anger, others with despair. Quite a number are consumed with the future, more than a few with regrets for the past, and a hefty percentage with worries about the present.

The good news is this: Jesus meets us where we are and does what he believes is best for us at the time.

It turns out the psalmist was right when he wrote, "Where can I go from your spirit? Or where can I flee from your presence? If I ascend to heaven, you are there; if I make my bed in Sheol, you are there" (Ps 139:7-8).

Christ, indeed, is with us. Christ, indeed, is with you.
And that is good news.

18

A Sower Goes on Sowing

Luke 8:1-21

I sat in the third pew, stage right one hot August night listening to our guest evangelist preach on the Parable of the Sower and the Seed.

He described in painstaking detail the four types of ground on which the seed fell: the hard path, shallow dirt scattered over a stone bed, thorn-infested earth, and good soil. Mopping sweat from his forehead with a large white handkerchief, he identified us with one of the four kinds of soil. He urged us to choose to be good soil, a person in whom the gospel might take root and flourish. And, it being a revival meeting, he urged us to make a once-for-all decision that night as we sang a hymn of invitation.

I have nothing negative to say about the evangelist or his sermon. He spoke from within a long-established interpretative tradition that tied the Scripture passage to a revival meeting's focus on immediate decision. And, no doubt, many of us made decisions that launched us into some form of the Christian life.

I did.

Jesus, though, had something more nuanced in mind when he told the Parable of the Sower and the Seed. Nowadays, when I consider the parable, I find that it speaks of the Christian life as I've come to experience it.

Start with the sower. Jesus tells of a sower who keeps on sowing, sling-ing seed across all the ground available to him. It's a strangely hopeful, some might say naive, way of sowing seed. Personally, if I knew where the deep, rich soil was to be found, I think I would sow seed there. Why waste good seed on unpromising ground?

Only, surely all of us realize Jesus was not talking about an actual farmer and his land. Jesus spoke of God, the kind of God who risks work-ing with everything present in each human life. God spreads the Spirit freely in hopes of reaping a harvest of life from some portion of our lives.

Now, as I move into my early sixties, I better comprehend the sheer grace-filled willingness of God to work with me as I am.

Pastors spend time with people. Over the years, I've found myself in many conversations that have fallen into a similar pattern.

"So, how might I be of help?" I say.

"I don't know," comes the reply. "I just feel like I'm failing God and everyone."

"Unpack that a bit for me," I respond.

"Okay. It's like this. I feel as if God is wasting his time on me. I mean, I know God wants me to get past my past. I'm pretty sure it would be good for me if I did. But I just can't do it! I don't see why God bothers with me when I can't seem to become the person God wants me to become."

Sometimes—not always, but sometimes—I've learned the best response I can offer is this: "Okay. Let's try something. Let's identify some part of your life in which God and you are working together well."

At that point, the two of us start the hard work of looking away from the part of a person's life that seems locked into a self-defeating pattern. Instead, we go in search of other areas in which God is making progress.

Almost always, though usually only after hard work, we find a few such areas. From that point on, I work with these people to help them learn to focus on the "fertile" ground in their lives, the parts of their lives in which the Jesus life is taking deep root.

When we do so, we may find the joy in Christ that so often eludes us. Please don't mistake me. Hard ground, rocky ground, shallow ground—all these remain. What I've learned, though, is that when the gospel takes deep root in any part of us, those roots spread over time, invade at least the edges of the hardened soils, and start to soften them from underneath.

Such has been the case for me.

I grew up in a home environment centered on alcoholism. A child who does so may react in any number of ways. In my case, I became wary of relationships, retreated into the world of my mind, and built a life designed around the goal of personal safety. To put it another way, I set out to become as independent of others as possible.

Looking back, I see that I sealed off large portions of myself. But one small portion of me remained open: my imagination, which I fed with stories from the Bible, classic mythologies, history, popular science, and modern works of fantasy. That's the ground in which the seed sown by God found entry, took root, and flourished.

That small piece of ground proved enough. It gave God a place from which to spread into all the other corners of my mind and heart. God went on working with me, even when only a very small part of me was open to God's work. And it was enough.

The same is true for all of us, including you. God never gives up. God goes on sowing, and the seed keeps on falling onto the various kinds of ground that constitute our lives.

Somewhere in your life, a few seeds are falling even now on fertile ground.

Find and work that ground! That's good enough work for today, and it's the kind of work that will bring a greater harvest than anyone can imagine in the days to come.

19

What Is Your Name?

Luke 8:22–56

Names matter.

The ancient Hebrews understood this better than we do. They took care with names, for names described or defined the one named. Abram the individual became Abraham, father of a multitude of nations, as a sign of the role he was to play in God's unfolding plan. Jacob, which means "usurper," became Israel, "one who strives with God." His new name described not only his evolving relationship with God but also his descendants' relationships to God. Simon became Peter, the rock, when Jesus designated Peter's confession of him as the Christ as the foundation on which the church would be built.

Names matter.

To lose one's name, then, is a horrific fate, for to it is to lose one's true self.

Luke tells the tale of an extreme case, a man possessed, a man who heard so many voices shouting and screaming their names in his mind that he could no longer remember his own name. On the day Jesus met him and asked him his name, the tomb dweller could only reply, "My name is Legion."

The man confesses himself at the mercy of all the clamoring names in his mind. Each seeks to define, describe, and direct him. First one then another seizes control of him for a while, only to be shoved aside by yet another.

Imagine some of the names vying to take charge of this man.

One voice almost certainly is called "Violence." When "Violence" holds sway, the man acts out the name. With unnatural strength, he breaks chains. No doubt he also lashes out at others and breaks relationships.

Perhaps another is called "Self-loathing." When "Self-loathing" runs the show, the man bruises and cuts himself with stones, lives naked and exposed to the elements, and seeks to destroy himself.

I suspect one of the names is "Despised by God." When this name takes charge, the man cannot imagine God loves him or wants anything to do with him.

One of the names, I think, is "Despair." When "Despair" rules, the man sees only that he must die and so goes and makes his home among the tombs of the dead.

On and on it goes. How many names seek to define him? "Legion" suggests one hundred. What we know for certain is that the poor man is overwhelmed by a host of false names. As long as they define him, he cannot find or be himself, even in the presence of Jesus.

That's why he cries out, "What have you to do with me, Jesus, Son of the Most High?" (v. 28).

Names matter.

Do you know that God gives us our true names the moment we come into this world?

Yes, I know parents or other caregivers name us. My own parents named me Michael, mostly because my mother liked the name and thought someone in the family ought to have it. She had no idea that its oldest form is Hebrew and means something like, "Who is like God?" It's a rhetorical question, of course, one meant to keep idolatry and overweening pride in check.

No one in my family knew the background of my name, but I hope I've lived into it so that's it's become a fair description of who I am and what I do.

Michael, though, is not my oldest and truest name. God gave me a name as well, the same one God gave you: "Beloved child of God." Each child born comes with that name. We all start life with a name that declares God's view of us: we are beloved children of God. That's our true name, the name that describes what we are meant to be and the family to which we belong.

Something then happens to all of us. Scriptures often label this something "the world." What does that mean? "The world" is a system of thought, economics, politics, family histories, and religion into which we are born. We live all our days in it. It's a system that tries to takes hold of us from our birth, and it succeeds. "The world" comes at us and attempts to make us forget our true name and take up other names.

Consider one example. Corporations, economic systems, advertisers, and governments rename us. They tell us, "Your name is Consumer. You are defined by what we can persuade you to want and spend; you are an economic measurement and nothing more." We too often buy into the name and start to think and act as if we are nothing more than a consumer. If we are not careful, we become incapable of discerning when we have enough or of taking satisfaction in enough. We devolve from being beloved children of God to being little more than devourers of goods, services, and the very stuff of the planet.

I can easily suggest other names the world attempts to give us: Liberal, Conservative, Advocate, Human Resource, Work Force, and the like. Surely, though, we get the picture.

Names matter. What name is the world trying to pin on you? What name are others attempting to assign you? What name is attempting to define you? Let's not settle for any name other than "Beloved Child of God."

Of course, we get into the game, too. We name others, thereby assigning them a place or role we think they have in the scheme of things.

Much of what we do is harmless for the most part. Lovers give one another nicknames. Friends often do the same.

But too often the names we give others do harm.

A tragic shooting in Charleston, South Carolina, is a case in point. Nine black people were murdered during a prayer meeting by a white man.

How do we explain such a thing? Racism, hatred, fear, and a host of other factors were clearly in play. Most of us, I hope, cannot fathom the mindset driving such actions.

I think names played a role.

The man who committed the murders had named his victims in various ways. To him, they were not people. Instead he labeled them a version of "Black," by which he meant subhuman. He named them "Enemy," by which he meant those who threatened his world. He labeled them "Problem," meaning something to be eliminated.

And so he entered a church facility on a Wednesday night and shot to death nine people he did not regard as fellow humans, let alone as beloved children of God.

Names matter.

They shape us. They define how we see ourselves and how we see others. The names we accept and the names we give form us, over time, into saints and sinners, into people who embody the love of God, or into people who embody pettiness, delusion, and hatred.

What are the names you use for other humans? Take care. The next time you find yourself labeling another person on the basis of race, sex, religion, relationships, nationality, politics, or family of origin, take a deep breath and back off. You don't want to go where such names will take you.

Names matter. Never settle for naming anyone else something less than "Beloved Child of God."

Jesus comes to the man who has lost his name, fallen victim to false names, and so lost his life. And Jesus heals him by banishing the false names.

What's the man's name? We're not told. All we know is that his right mind returns, and he puts on clothes and sits with Jesus.

Mind you, I don't doubt the man now remembers the name his parents gave him, but I don't think that's the name he embraces as he lingers with Jesus.

In that moment with Jesus, he knows his true name: "Beloved Child of God." He wants to hold on to it and never lose it again. That's why he is afraid when Jesus tells him to go back to his home territory and tell them his story. He fears he will again forget his true name, forget who and what he is.

I can't say I blame him. The "world" is always with us, and it never ceases to try to make us forget our true name and the true name of all others. Only a fool would not be at least a bit afraid.

I cannot give you an infallible method for remembering our shared true name, but I can offer an exercise I try to practice frequently. Perhaps it will help you.

I say the following words to myself: *Step today into the world as it is. Walk carefully. As you walk through this day, never settle for calling yourself by any name other than "Beloved Child of God." As you walk through this day, never settle for calling anyone else by any name other than "Beloved Child of God." Remember, names matter. Hold on to the name God gives to you and to all others.*

That's how I try to remember who I am, who you are, and who "they" are. With the help of God and others, it works.

What's your name? It turns out that the question matters more than we might have imagined. Jesus knows this is so, and it's well past time we know it, too.

20

Resetting Our Expectations about Life with Jesus

Luke 9:1–36

Each of us holds assumptions about Jesus. The longer we walk with him, the more we recognize, discard, or alter our assumptions. We're in good company. Those who spent the most time with Jesus during his pubic ministry had to shed their assumptions about what they would be and do as his followers.

There's little doubt that by this time, the disciples believed Jesus to be the long-anticipated Messiah. Along with such belief, they held a set of expectations about what they would receive as those closest to the Messiah.

To put it bluntly, they expected to be placed in charge, to serve as nobility within the royal court of the Messiah. They remind me of some American Christians who honestly (but erroneously) believe wealth, money, and power are the rewards Christ gives his followers.

I think the disciples were surprised the day Jesus told them to hit the road to proclaim the kingdom of God and minister to the sick, taking only the clothes on their backs and accepting whatever hospitality (or lack of it) they encountered. Such work bore little resemblance to what they had expected to do as followers of Jesus. Still, according to Luke they proved effective at the assigned task. They returned to Jesus and told him all they had done.

Even so, I don't think they grasped the import of the experience. Sure, they all returned safely, some people were healed, and a few no doubt even joined the larger band of disciples. But even as Jesus took the apostles away on a retreat, I suspect they went expecting him to say, "Well done. You've laid the groundwork for what comes next. Now that the people have seen you do some of what I've been doing, they'll better accept you as my surrogates in greater matters. It's almost time to mount your thrones, my friends, and rule in my name!"

Jesus, instead, dragged them into even more ministry work. When a large crowd found their retreat site, Jesus spent the entire day teaching and healing those who needed such care.

Finally, the long day drew to a close, and the disciples tried to assume the role of royal advisors. They clustered around Jesus and said, "Send the crowd away, so that they may go into the surrounding villages and countryside, to lodge and get provisions" (v. 12). No doubt, they expected Jesus to agree and send them out among the people with the message.

Instead, he staggered them by responding, "You give them something to eat" (v. 13).

We've heard versions of the story so many times that I'm afraid we seldom feel the impact of Jesus' statement on his disciples. They were tired. I suspect they were more than a little irritated that Jesus chose to minister to the crowd rather than conduct a private retreat with them. Now, just when they thought they might get some time with him, Jesus told them they were not done with the crowd and gave them an impossible task.

They responded just as we would: "It can't be done. We can't feed five thousand men plus all the women and children. All we've got is five small pieces of bread and two little fish. Why, that's hardly a meal for Peter, let alone enough to feed the crowd."

How easily we assume that the limits of our resources determine what Jesus can accomplish. The disciples were about to learn a lesson all of us need to absorb: a little is a lot in the hands of Jesus.

Jesus took what they actually had available, blessed it, and proceeded to do what was needed: he fed each person present and wound up with leftovers.

A little is a lot in the hands of Jesus. I required years to hear, assimilate, and accept that reality. Most Christians do. I'm not talking about the kind of superficial and self-serving form of Christianity that often tells us to "name and claim it." It's not that Christ tells us to identify what we want and he will give it to us!

No, indeed. He sends us out to minister with only the shirts on our backs.

But when Jesus says, "Feed the poor," he will provide resources for the ministry as we undertake to perform it. When Jesus says, "Become peacemakers in a world given to violence," he will take our meager resources and multiply their impact as we work for peace.

Get the idea? If Jesus tells his people to do something, they are best advised to take whatever they already have on hand and get started.

Long years ago, a minister and physician named Scott felt God prodding him to start a ministry to the working poor of Memphis, Tennessee. Scott did not know how he might provide space and money for such a ministry, but he chose to get started. Soon a church made some of its unused facilities available.

A volunteer or two came along. Some individuals and foundations became interested. Eventually hospitals, medical and dental practices, and a host of volunteers came on board. Today in Memphis, The Church Health Center provides high-quality care to thousands of patients per year—all because Scott laid aside the assumptions that might have prevented him from taking on the task Christ gave him. Scott learned that a little is a lot in the hands of Jesus.

Back to the disciples. Sometime after the feeding of the crowd, Jesus began to ask his disciples who they thought he was. Eventually, Peter—speaking for the others—answered, "The Messiah of God" (v. 20). Jesus then told them a truth: those who would follow him must lay aside any assumption that the way would be cost free or even conventionally profitable. They were to take up their crosses, that is, discard their previous expectations of safety and personal gain. If they would do so, they would come to experience the Jesus kind of life during their lifetimes.

Finally, Jesus took Peter, James, and John to a mountaintop where they experienced the Transfiguration. They caught a glimpse of the glory of Jesus. Toward the end of the experience, just as Peter started trying to tell Jesus what to do, the very voice of God spoke from a cloud: "This is my Son, my Chosen; listen to him" (v. 33).

There we have it: the last assumption to put away is that we can tell Jesus what to be or do in God's world. In its place, we must learn to "listen" to what Jesus has to say. Peter and his fellow apostles would spend the rest of their days trying to learn to do so.

What are our assumptions about life with Jesus? Try naming yours. Can our assumptions stand when measured against the expectations of Jesus? If not, isn't it time to reset our expectations?

We know it's time to do so. Let's get started now.

21

The Day After

Luke 9:37–62

If not for the stories of the disciples the day after the Transfiguration, I might think I'm the only one who struggles to follow Jesus well. Thank goodness for Luke's honesty as he tells their story.

As the saying goes, "You can't make this stuff up." In the space of a day, the disciples botch a healing, boggle at the thought that Jesus must suffer and die, compete for prominence in the kingdom of God, and presume to be judge and executioner in the name of Jesus.

We're tempted to think them incredibly dense and self-centered, aren't we? How could people living in daily contact with Jesus continue to be so mired in cultural expectations, self-centeredness, prejudice, and the like?

The sad but true answer is they continued to fail in such ways because they were like us.

Take, for example, the power of prejudice compounded with self-interest to derail discipleship. James and John, according to other Gospel accounts, yearn to be named the chief lieutenants of Jesus. No doubt they also share their culture's prejudice against Samaritans. When a Samaritan village refuses to receive Jesus, the brothers respond to the insult in ways conditioned by their ambitions and bigotry. It's as if they've not experienced the Jesus who talked and modeled forgiveness toward enemies and toward those who treated one with disrespect.

Isn't that how it is with us? Not too long ago, a group of Christian men in our church spent most of a day studying the Sermon on the Mount. They wrestled with the implications of Jesus' words. Later some of the men in the group stood talking outside the building. The topic of immigration came up. Immediately several in the group began to speak of immigrants in harsh terms.

Finally, one of the men brought the conversation to a halt when he said, "I'm ashamed of myself, guys. Here I stand having just studied the words of Jesus about neighbors, treating others as I want to be treated, and such. Yet over the last few moments, I've been talking as if I've never heard of Jesus. I've sounded more like my old, reactionary uncle than Jesus."

The truth is, it's not easy to follow Jesus well, even on the day after the Transfiguration, let alone on the other days of the week.

Let's not give up. Jesus, though disappointed in his disciples, does not send them away. Instead, he corrects them and takes them on with him. I suppose he thinks—or, at least hopes—they may yet learn his way if they keep traveling with him.

Eventually, most of them do, though only at great cost. Our hope and prayer is that the same may one day be said of us.

22

Sent Out

Luke 10:1-24

Long-distance hikers learn to travel light. Those who don't soon turn to other forms of recreation.

Luke tells the story of the day Jesus sent seventy of his followers out on the road to take his kind of ministry to the people. Apparently, Jesus believed his followers had to go where people lived rather than wait for folks to come to them.

By now, most of his followers were seasoned travelers. They thought they knew what items and attitudes they ought to take on a journey. Jesus' instructions challenged their assumptions.

He told them to take no money, bag, or shoes. Furthermore, they were not to reserve rooms with friends or innkeepers or anyone else. Instead, he told them to keep on the move, stay with whoever might welcome them, and eat whatever someone might offer. In the event they found no welcome, they were to move on to the next village and try again.

Apparently, Jesus believed such an approach would free his followers to focus on task rather than comfort.

Suffice it to say that a healing ministry in the first century probably addressed the most frightening aspect of human life in that era. Most in that time believed disease was the result of sin and/or demonic activity. They must have felt helpless in the face of the inscrutable illness in their lives. A healing ministry injected hope into their lives and made real the possibility that the kingdom of God had come near them.

Many pastors and scholars have spoken eloquently on the power of the seventy's ministry, but today I'm most interested in Jesus' travel instructions. Are they relevant for the church and individual Christian today?

We hear a great deal these days about churches disconnecting from people in their community and wider culture. Even a casual Internet search produces a long list of articles on the irrelevant, declining, or dying church.

Quite a number of authors and consultants provide suggestions on how to rectify the situation. I'm grateful for the good work done by many of them.

Until we can arrange for such folks to help us, though, here's what I think Jesus would have us do: Get out among all sorts of people, travel light, do some good, point to God, and keep moving. Learn along the way. Gather together every now and then with God and one another, share our experiences, give thanks to God, and head back out there.

Anyone up for a road trip?

23

Reshape Your Life

Luke 10:25-37

"What must I do to inherit eternal life?" asks the lawyer (v. 25), by which he means, "What must I do to know and have the kind of life God wants for me?"

That's a first-rate question, isn't it? Indeed, it's the one question into which all other questions must be folded.

Interestingly, the one asking the question already knows the answer: love God with everything you've got, and love your neighbor as yourself. By the time of Jesus, there's no longer much debate over the answer. Call it settled theology. What must we do to have the kind of life God wants for us? I suspect many of us also know the answer: practice full and unreserved love toward God and all others.

If the lawyer and we already know the answer, what's the point in asking the question? Ah, now we get to the heart of the matter. First-century Jews did not doubt the need to love God wholly and one's neighbor as one's self. They debated instead the limits of "neighbor." The lawyer's second question reflects the debate: "And who is my neighbor?" (v. 29). Did neighbor mean only one's family member, a fellow Jewish person, a person who belonged to one's particular sect within Judaism, or something more? Their debate assumed one could love God fully yet set limits on the meaning of neighbor. Some even assumed the full love of God might require them to set such limits.

This sounds like some of what I hear in our time. Just how far does neighbor go? Does neighbor include all Christians, Jews, Muslims, the poor, the addicted, criminals, other races . . . (the list goes on and on)?

I don't think I've ever known a Christian who doubted we were to love God with all our heart, mind, soul, and strength (v. 27). With regret, however, I've heard many Christians declare certain individuals and people groups off limits.

When we try to set limits on whom we regard and treat as our neighbor, we distance ourselves from God and the life God intends for us. Jesus packaged such a perspective in a story we call The Parable of the Good Samaritan.

We know the story. A man sets out on the road only to be waylaid by bandits who beat, strip, and rob him. We're told nothing about his ethnic or religious identity. As he lies by the road, a Pharisee and priest pass by. Each walks on, leaving the man to his fate.

Finally, a Samaritan happens by. First-century Jews assumed Samaritans were thieves and untrustworthy. Those listening to the story would expect the Samaritan to check to see if the man had anything left to steal! Instead, the Samaritan rescues the victim, installs him at an inn, tends to his wounds, and makes provision for his continued care.

When Jesus asks the lawyer which person was a neighbor to the man, he has little choice but to respond, "The one who showed him mercy" (v. 37). And Jesus responds, "Go and do likewise" (v. 37).

Jesus assumes it's possible for the lawyer—and us—to go and do likewise. How? What must we do to reshape ourselves into "Good Samaritans"?

Based on the story and long years of walking alongside Christians who seek to do so, I've learned we must reshape ourselves in at least four ways.

First, we must reframe our vision. Imagine yourself as the victim. How would you feel? What would you hope? You'd hope that someone would stop and help you. Learning to see through the eyes of another helps us move toward becoming Good Samaritans. The priest and the Levite see the victim as someone outside the scope of their concern and as someone to be avoided for the sake of theological and practical safety. The Samaritan sees the victim as a fellow human he can and should help.

I've found a sentence prayer useful to help me foster a Good Samaritan way of seeing others, and I offer it for your use: "O Christ, change the way I see all others; reshape my vision so that I see them as you see them."

Second, we must reshape our values and goals. The priest and the Levite represented the best and brightest among God's ancient people, but it's hard to see how their values and goals differed from those of a typical Roman or Greek of the era. They appeared to value personal safety, taking care of their own, drawing theological lines of acceptance and non-acceptance, or perhaps just getting home after a hard day's work more than they valued the life of the victim. The Samaritan would have been expected to have similar or lesser values. Instead, the Samaritan chose to stop, help, and go on helping.

Ask yourself, what are my values and goals? Do they match up with Christ's insistence that I love all others as I love myself? Again, I've found a sentence prayer useful to help me focus on the challenge. The prayer goes like this: "O Christ, examine and tear down any of my values and goals that get in the way of loving others as I love myself."

Third, we must reshape our relationships. The priest and Levite lived in what I suspect they would have called the real world, a world in which relationships were set in stone by custom or religion. In their "real world," boundaries were clear-cut. They assumed their relationship boundaries were God's as well. In their eyes, it was wrong to step over such boundaries.

The Samaritan broke all the established relationship rules. He befriended a stranger whose ethnic and religious background he did not know. He entered into a short- and long-term relationship with the victim. Jesus said God approved the Samaritan's approach to the victim and wanted it to become normative for God's people.

When is the last time you stepped over a relationship boundary to act as a neighbor, to enter deliberately into a relationship with someone who did not already fit into your world?

Here's a sentence prayer to help: "O Christ, send me someone to befriend from outside my established circles of acceptable people."

Fourth, we must reshape our behavior. The priest and Levite acted in ways most people in their time would have approved. The Samaritan broke through established behaviors to do a new thing. He did so, though no one else might have approved or understood and though his actions might have cost him safety, time, and money.

Jesus approved the behavior of the Good Samaritan, and his endorsement holds implications for us.

What might we do? Look for someone in need in your family, school, workplace, community, or the larger world. Once you spot someone, you've probably found your starting point. Link up with others who are trying to cross boundaries and be good neighbors to others. (It's good to have company!)

Consider using the following sentence prayer frequently: "O Christ, give me no peace until I start to take loving actions toward all the kinds of people I find in the world."

Loving and treating others as we would have them love and treat us is the way of Jesus. Let's reshape our lives accordingly.

24

How to Find Your Focus

Luke 10:38-42

The story of Jesus, Mary, and Martha delights or infuriates us. There seems to be no middle ground.

Jesus continues on his way. That is, he keeps moving not only in terms of geography but also of his mission. He and the disciples enter the village where Martha and Mary live. John's Gospel tells us Martha, Mary, and their brother Lazarus are good friends of Jesus. Naturally, Jesus accepts Martha's offer of lodging and food.

The disciples troop to Martha's house, and tensions soon rise.

Martha goes into overdrive as she welcomes the group, makes them comfortable, and sets about preparing food for all of them. Meanwhile, her sister Mary plops down on the floor at the feet of Jesus and listens as he teaches.

After a while, a thoroughly irritated Martha interrupts Jesus with a direct question: "Lord, don't you care that my sister has left me to do all the work? Tell her to help me!" (v. 40, paraphrase).

My best guess is that the male disciples agree with Martha. The probably think it's high time for someone to intervene. No doubt they believe it inappropriate for a woman to be directly taught by Jesus in company with men. More than a few of them probably think Jesus should long ago have sent Mary off to do "woman's work."

I wonder if Mary expects Jesus to send her away once Martha raises the issue. After all, such an action fits all cultural expectations.

Martha and the disciples are surprised, even a little scandalized, when Jesus replies, "Martha, Martha, you are worried and upset about many things, but one thing is needed. Mary has chosen what is better, and it will not be taken from her" (v. 41, paraphrase).

Luke practices a discreet silence about what comes next, but I suspect the atmosphere in the house grew distinctly chilly, and I rather doubt Martha offered Jesus second helpings at dinner.

The story is about focus, about where we choose to invest ourselves. It is not a story about good versus evil. Rather, it deals with a daily, all-too-Christian quandary: How are we to stay focused on Jesus in the face of competing, interesting, and even useful options? The story calls us to find and keep a sharp focus on Jesus.

The more I ponder the story, the more I think about how we might lose focus on Jesus. Most of us begin our journey with Jesus determined to pay close attention to him. If we are honest, though, we must confess that we often lose focus.

Why? To put it gently, we are highly distractible.

My wife and I own (or are owned by) a black Labrador retriever named Stella. Stella loves both of us, misses us when we are away, and keeps an eye on us. She wants to do whatever we're doing.

Truth be told, though, she is highly distractible. Even when we're playing her favorite game of fetch the ball, her focus wanders. A firefly, the wind rustling some leaves, a bird flying overhead, and—of course—a squirrel easily divert her attention. Immediately, she shifts her focus, and it's as if my wife and I don't exist.

I am not calling any of us Labrador retrievers, but we are distractible.

Almost anything can distract us. I don't have to think long to make a list of examples. Television, politics, recreation activities, and sports come easily to mind. I've known people so caught up in planning activities, settling old scores, helping others in various ways, managing money, rearing children, running a business, or planning worship services that they lose sight of Jesus, forget to listen to what he is saying, and fail to walk closely with him.

Martha's story reveals the dynamics of our distractibility.

Like Martha, we get swept up in culturally mandated or approved tasks. When others do not follow suit, we fall into self-pity and self-righteous anger. We start to try to force others to share our jumbled priorities.

If we're not careful, we may find ourselves emulating Martha, who became so agitated that she interrupted Jesus and tried to enlist him in her cause. Actually, she went further. Martha expected Jesus to see the error of his way, repent, and get with her program!

Framed this way, Martha's expectations seem a little overreaching.

The good news is that we need not settle for living driven by a misplaced or skewed focus. We can find or rediscover our focus on Jesus.

I assume we want to do so. Am I correct? Do you want to turn your eyes to Jesus, tune your ears to Jesus, set your feet to walking with Jesus? If so, once again the story points the way.

Invite Jesus into your space. Martha made a good start when she invited Jesus and his disciples to her house.

Sit at his feet. Mary got it right. When Jesus comes to your place and starts to speak, settle down and listen. Do so in the context of your place, your life as it actually is at this point in time.

Resist the lure of useful busyness. Let the kettle boil over and the bread burn. Choose to give Jesus your full attention. Lay down the cell phone, turn off the television, and step out of your overscheduled routine. Nothing you might do—even if it might actually be useful—is as important as listening when Jesus is speaking.

Place the agenda solely in the hands of Jesus. Martha tried to set the agenda, and in doing so she followed the natural pattern of things. After all, she issued the invitation and therefore felt responsible for the rest and nourishment of her guests. Only—and it's a big "only"—Jesus was not her usual guest. Jesus came into the house wanting to speak and teach all those who were within the reach of his voice, including Martha and Mary.

He still does so. Don't worry. When Jesus is ready for you or me to get up and go do something else, he will let us know.

What comes next for you and me? What will we do with the story?

I know from experience that many of us will want to carry on Martha's argument for her. Don't give in to the temptation to do so. Each time we succumb, we set ourselves against Jesus.

Others of us will worry a bit: "Well, if I follow Mary's lead, nothing will get done." We're wrong. Those who follow Mary's way ultimately become the kind of people who take the gospel to the world. Something comes first, though. We start by focusing on listening to Jesus.

The best action we can take is to deliberately take our place at the feet of Jesus and listen to whatever he may have to say. Remember, such a focus is the best way, the way that never can be taken from us unless we ourselves surrender it.

If we want to stay focused on Jesus, we must choose the way of Mary. Let it be so.

25

The Shape of Prayer

Luke 11:1–13

A friend of mine named Tom Steagald wrote a book with a great title: *Praying for Dear Life*. The title is apt. Prayer is the key to the life of a Christian and the life of the church.

That being so, the shape of prayer matters. Why? The shape of prayer shapes us. Jesus knew this to be so, and he provided a shaping prayer, one version of which is found in Luke's Gospel.

Rightly shaped prayer teaches us to step consciously into the presence of God.

We know all life is lived in the presence of God, but that's not easy to remember. Prayer is the means by which we practice living each moment in the presence of God. Good prayer helps form us into women and men who intentionally live in the presence of God.

Rightly shaped prayer mixes intimacy and awe.

Jesus squeezed together two perspectives in his model prayer: intimacy with God and awe before God. He spoke to God as a small child might speak to a loving parent, one the child trusts without reservation. Yet he also acknowledged God as the one who exceeds our comprehension.

Over the course of a lifetime, prayer turns us into people who feel able to trust God without falling into the trap of thinking we've got God boxed in, figured out, or at our beck and call.

We become like a small child who loves and trusts her parents so much that there is no hesitation to talk freely with them, admit ignorance, or even confess failure. That same child, though, over time also comes to understand that parents have a life beyond that of the child, one that will always remain something of a mystery and that merits respect.

Rightly shaped prayer leads us to yearn for God's rule.

Many people in the first century spoke of yearning for God's rule to take effect. But what they meant was, "May the day soon come when the world is run the way I think it should be run and when people just like me are in charge. May the day soon come when God sees things my way and makes the world march to my beat."

We often exhibit the same kind of confusion between our will and the will of God.

Jesus' prayer works to shape us into people who trust and revere God enough to yearn for God's will to be done in us and the world at large, even if God's will turns out to be quite different from what we expect.

Such prayer molds us so that we increasingly want to know what God wants us to do with our time, energy, money, relationships, skills, and gifts. We become, over time, people who wish to share God's dream for God's world. Our resistance to God crumples, and our openness to God becomes deeper and more profound.

Rightly shaped prayer refashions and limits our desires.

Can you imagine becoming a person who wants less and less? If we practice the kind of prayer Jesus provides, such a thing happens.

The prayer draws on the exodus experience, especially God's provision of manna. God sent just enough manna for a day, and when anyone tried to hoard more, it decayed and melted away.

Do you suppose God was unable to provide food preservatives? Of course not! God used the daily portion ration to drive home a point: God's people depend on God for their daily needs.

Prayer, at its best, shapes us into such people. We increasingly are freed from the tyranny of things and so freed to follow God wherever God may lead.

The struggle of Christians not to succumb to the tyranny of things may be the greatest challenge of our era (at least in the United States). Certainly praying only for daily provision is a hard discipline. Let's do it anyway.

Rightly shaped prayer reminds us of our need for forgiveness and our God-given ability to ask for it.

We become people who frequently acknowledge our need for forgiveness and better discern the obvious and subtle ways in which sin works in us. Through prayer, we grow secure enough in God's love to confess each discovery.

That's a good thing! The more we move in such a direction, the more we start to enjoy freedom from hypocrisy, guilt, and fear.

Rightly shaped prayer prompts us to upgrade our treatment of those who have sinned against us. We become people who freely give forgiveness.

Jesus taught that those who cannot forgive are unable to fully experience the joy and freedom of receiving forgiveness. When we project our own unforgiving nature onto God, we soon harbor doubts about being forgiven by God. The only way to come to believe in the full power of forgiveness is to practice forgiving others.

This is hard, very hard, for others often seem undeserving of forgiveness, do not know how to ask for it, and sometimes abuse it. God knows this is so, yet God forgives. In Christ, God calls us to become the kind of people who can follow God's lead.

Rightly shaped prayer deepens our humility with regard to our limits.

Prayer reins in our pride, teaching us we are not strong or wise enough to face evil alone. It helps us see that any of us can be broken.

We learn to pray that God will spare us from trials or tests, and we ask to be shielded from more than we may be able to endure. At the same time, we acknowledge that God may send a test our way in order to help us grow spiritual muscle and serve God better, but we never seek such.

Learning and praying the Lord's Prayer is crucial to the healthy Christian life. I've found it useful to recast this prayer in my own words, as I try to appropriate its shaping power. The prayer goes as follows:

Help me, Lord, to choose to live always aware of your presence. Teach me to trust you without reservation. Remind me that you are not a tame God. Fill me with a deep yearning for your way of life. Curb my runaway desires, that I might be free to follow you. Lead me to accept your forgiveness. Prod me to forgive others, even as you forgive me. Show me my limits, and help me live within them. Amen.

26

Can We See What Is in Front of Us?

Luke 11:14-36

During my fifth grade year, the local Lion's Club paid a visit to our school. They came to offer free eye exams, no small thing in our relatively poor rural area. The Lion's Club enlisted a number of women to help administer the test, including my mother.

Mom set up the equipment, had me take my place, and started the examination. Following time-honored procedures, she showed me sets of slides and asked me which seemed clearer to me.

Slide followed slide. To my mother's consternation, I kept saying, more or less, "I can't see much of anything." She got angry and told me to stop goofing off. I told her I was doing my best and telling the truth. Finally, she called for help. An optometrist who had volunteered for the day took her place and started the test over. In response to his questions, I gave the same answer I had given my mother: "I can't see much of anything."

Suffice it to say that by the time we finished, we knew I had poor eyesight. The machine and the exam cards were fine. The problem lay with me. I honestly could not see what was right in front of my eyes.

Not too long thereafter, I put on my first pair of prescription glasses, saw things I'd never before noticed, and my life changed. I can't claim much credit. The Lion's Club, my mother, and a skilled optometrist drove the process. All I did was answer their questions as honestly as I could and cooperate.

All of which combines to shift my perspective on Luke 11:14-36. Once I automatically disdained those who opposed Jesus, accused him of being in league with the devil, or simply could not perceive he was the promised Messiah. Now, though, I tend to feel for them. After all, I once could not see what was right before my eyes. Perhaps they were well intentioned yet could not see.

The moment I allow for such a possibility, my interpretation of Jesus' interaction with them shifts, too. Is he angry as he tells the little parable of the strong man or draws on the Jonah story, or is he simply trying to help them see what is in front of their eyes? The latter option seems likely.

I'm struck by how hard Jesus works to open their eyes. The longer I ponder the story, the more I'm driven to wonder how well I see God at work in the world around me. What might God be doing in my congregation, neighborhood, family, social circles, and the world at large that I simply do not see? Am I willing to try to allow God to open my eyes and help me see? Are you?

I hope so. I really hope so.

27

A Self-test

Luke 11:37–12:3

Like many of us, I have a few recurring nightmares about high school and college.

In one of them, I'm taking a test I must pass before being permitted to graduate. Just as I complete and hand in the test, I realize I'm in the wrong room and that I don't know the professor. I've taken the wrong test and blown my chance to graduate! Usually, I wake up shaken, look about my bedroom, and slowly talk myself out of despair.

Imagine how it would feel to be told you had been taking the wrong test all your life with regard to your relationship with God? If you can imagine this, you will begin to appreciate Luke 11:34-54.

The Pharisee believed he and his colleagues were taking the correct self-test. If they passed, they would fashion lives pleasing to God. It was a long test, and they needed to get all the answers right.

Their test is too long to survey, but a few examples suffice to demonstrate its characteristics. They had to be careful to tithe every conceivable asset to the Lord: cash, profits, produce, various herbs, and the like. Careful practice of a host of ritual cleansings mattered, too.

While not part of the official test, many Pharisees thought it important to win public acknowledgment as masters of the law and as "pure" individuals. Some took such public opinion as the measure of their standing with God.

They thought they had the God/human relationship figured out, that they knew the right questions and the right answers. Jesus challenged their assumptions by omitting a cleansing ritual they regarded as vital: he and his disciples did not wash their hands before eating a meal.

Let's be clear about what was at stake: a religious ritual the Pharisees considered important, one they assumed to be part of the self-test one had to pass to honor and please God. They were astonished that Jesus failed to observe the ritual.

Jesus discerned their thoughts. Rather than quail before their disapproval, he demolished their premise with a few well-chosen words.

Jesus said any self-test that stresses outward signs of purity while leaving one's heart and mind unclean is worthless. One's standing with God was not improved by tithing, winning the approval of fellow Pharisees, discovering ever more minute ways to apply the law, or guarding traditions against God-inspired reformation. In short, the Pharisees' self-test was based on a mistaken notion of what God sought.

The Pharisees did not take kindly to Jesus' words. As Luke puts it, "When Jesus left there, the Pharisees and teachers of the law began to oppose him fiercely."

No one likes to be told they've been wrong about what it takes to enjoy God's approval, including us! I'm afraid we have much in common with the Pharisees in the story. Baptist history (why pick on someone else?) offers plenty of examples. What words might Jesus say to Baptists, for example? I can imagine him saying something along the following lines.

> *Now, then, you Baptists wash up really nicely in your baptismal pools, but inside you remain full of yourselves, given to greed and pettiness and self-protectiveness. It's often hard to distinguish you from business sharks, political operatives, and religious inquisitors.*
>
> *Woe to you Baptists, for though as a people you give a great deal of money for many things, you often neglect simple justice and the love of God.*
>
> *Woe to you Baptists, for you love your special places at covered-dish suppers and your coveted leadership titles in the church.*
>
> *Woe to you Baptists, for you nearly always resist any new movement of Holy Spirit in favor of holding on to what you already have. You even exile those who dare disturb your little kingdoms.*
>
> *Woe to you Baptists, for you too often add to the burdens of people who yearn to know, love, and serve God.*
>
> *Woe to you Baptists, for you have lost your way yet continue to act as if you know the way.*

See what I mean? Such language makes us angry. The more specific the language gets, the more we are tempted to go the way of the Pharisees and oppose whoever challenges us, even Jesus. We act as if Jesus himself does not have the right to challenge the self-tests we've developed and approved.

Perhaps, though, we can do better. Might we choose to listen to the Holy Spirit, as the Spirit asks us to set aside resentment, learn from Jesus, accept what he says, and allow him to reset our goals? How ought the people of God measure ourselves? Jesus gave clear answers.

Face and deal with the ungodly stuff inside us. Stop focusing on policing others. Instead, spend our energies on discerning and repenting of our own sins and opening ourselves to God's forgiveness.

Help the poor. Jesus made doing so an important part of our self-evaluation. Anyone who thinks they are living a God-approved lifestyle without helping the poor is caught up in delusion. Feeding, clothing, sheltering, teaching, and ministering to the poor is hard and unending work. Nonetheless, God demands his people take up the task.

Support the ongoing work of the people of God. Jesus endorsed tithing to the temple and synagogue and, by extension, the church. He knew tithing forces us to think about our resources, how to use them well, and how they fit into our relationship with God.

Demand and work for justice for all people. In the first century, as in our own time, those with the least tended to receive the least from the justice and economic systems. Like all the prophets, Jesus insisted that God's people practice and work for equal justice for all.

Nurture your love for God. Jesus did not propose earning salvation by good works; instead, he insisted that good works are a product of loving God. He stressed that God's people must tend their love for God, lest it grow cold due to exhaustion and the distractions of life. This is why we come again and again to God through worship, prayer, study, and reflection. We do such things not to win God's approval but to help us make God the center of our lives.

Watch for and support new movements of God's Spirit. I think this is hard in any era. Jesus insists that we measure ourselves by our willingness to look and see where God is at work in fresh ways to accomplish God's eternal objectives: drawing people to God, strengthening the knowledge and love of God, challenging power systems that demean or hurt people, and binding God's people to one another.

Place nothing in the way of those who would follow God. The religious leaders of Jesus' day placed heavy burdens on those who wished to live a life approved by God. They thought themselves keepers of the door to the house of salvation. Jesus said such self-appointed doorkeepers did not even have a key to the door! Rather than set ourselves up as doorkeepers, let's choose to follow the model of Jesus. He pointed to God, welcomed anyone who wanted to try to walk with God, and left judgment to God.

Start taking the right test. Learn to ask yourself a few questions again and again. Am I dealing with my own sin, helping the poor, centering my economic life on God, working for justice for all people, nurturing my love for God, welcoming God's new movements, and working hard not to place obstacles of any kind in the way of anyone who wishes to follow Jesus?

Fair warning: living into such an ongoing test will reshape you. You will experience real, sometimes drastic changes in your beliefs, attitudes, and actions. Not everyone will approve.

God will, and that's enough for any Christ follower.

Live as if There Is a God

Luke 12:4-13:9

My fraternal grandmother once said something that fixed itself in my memory. A man who worked as a day laborer on the family farm had made a series of bad decisions which combined to place himself and his family at risk. Some of the other farm workers gathered on the farmhouse front porch after lunch and fell to talking about their colleague. Frankly, they said some rather harsh things about him.

My grandmother shushed them and said, "He's not a bad man. He's just afraid. All of us are apt to fail God and ourselves when we're afraid." The workers murmured, "Yes, Mrs. Belle," and headed back to the fields. I don't know what they thought of her comment. To me, it sounded like something worth remembering, though I would need years of life experience to appreciate the depth of her insight.

"All of us are apt to fail God and ourselves when we are afraid." The adage helps us appropriate and apply Luke 12:4–13:9.

Jesus insists that fear drains our capacity to live as if there is a God in whom we can trust. He goes on to give example after example of the debilitating effects of fear. Fear drives us to . . .

. . . forget God is watching over us.

. . . live and speak in ways that deny we know Christ.

. . . back away from affirming the work God is doing and even allow such work to be called evil.

. . . invest time and energy in worrying about how to defend ourselves against attack.

. . . seek security by accumulating stuff.

. . . try to take over the world and run it for our material benefit.

. . . ignore the signals God sends to call us to abandon fear in favor of trust in God.

. . . build ourselves up by focusing on the sins of others.

Like my grandmother said, "All of us are apt to fail God and ourselves when we are afraid."

Don't you think it's time you and I tried something quite different, in fact attempted the very thing Jesus describes? He tells us to live each moment as if we believe God never forgets us and to invest ourselves in striving for the kingdom of God.

A few years ago, I developed a short, easy-to-remember phrase that helps me resist structuring my life around fear and reframe my life around trust in God. The phrase goes like this: "Live as if there is a God."

When I'm on top of my game (which is less often than I care to admit), I take the phrase with me into the arenas of my life. I find it makes quite a difference to my thought process, feelings, conclusions, and actions. I start to ask myself how the matter before me might be used to test and deepen my trust in God or advance the goals of God (if you've forgotten the goals, see the sermon of Jesus at Nazareth in Luke 4). I go on to ask myself what I might do if I actually chose to embrace God's goals without fear.

Living as if there is a God is the key to building a life and society more nearly in accordance with God's dream.

If you and I are prepared to make the attempt, God stands ready to support us.

The Woman Who Did Not Fit

Luke 13:10-17

We love to stuff things into boxes, and that's all right when it comes to items such as books, clothes, dishes, and knickknacks. The problem is that we sometimes try to place people and even God in a box. Doing so never works out well.

There's a story in Luke's Gospel about this kind of thing, a tale set in a synagogue on a Sabbath morning.

Jesus is teaching, and it's hard work. Even though the people and the synagogue leader no doubt insist they want to learn, the truth is that they mostly want Jesus to reinforce what they already believe and practice. In that respect, we have much in common.

As it turns out, he will teach them not only on the basis of Scripture but also through an unanticipated incident.

Luke says a woman appears. I find the phrase interesting. Luke makes it sound as if she suddenly popped into existence. Most likely, he means us to realize no one noticed her until that moment.

I think that's probably true at a functional level. She has been among them for eighteen years, bent over painfully from a disease no one could diagnose. Over the years, she has faded into the background, become part of the scenery, and so goes unnoticed.

She's a woman, and as such she has little standing in the synagogue, at least in the eyes of the men who lead it. The woman is functionally invisible to them.

I wonder how the woman feels. Eighteen years is a long time. How does she feel as she observes the Sabbath and comes to the synagogue? Has she made peace with her illness and her virtual invisibility? Does she come still hoping something might happen to change her life for the better, or has she grown so accustomed to her illness and place in the community that she cannot imagine the possibility of anything better?

She lives in a box, hemmed in by others and her condition, a box I suspect she has begun to treat as the only home she will ever know. And she might be correct, except that on this particular day Jesus is on the scene.

Jesus breaks all the rules in the space of a few moments. He notices the woman and calls her over to him. Jesus does so in an environment where it is assumed men must not notice or speak to women in public. By calling her to himself, Jesus invites the woman to leave the assigned place for women in the synagogue and join him in an area typically reserved for males.

When Jesus heals her, he adds to his list of offenses. Healing is defined as work, and as such is forbidden on the Sabbath, let alone in the synagogue on the Sabbath.

The woman straightens up for the first time in eighteen years. Imagine how slowly she moves, almost afraid to believe, worried the old pain might strike and force her back down. Finally, she stands up straight. Suddenly, she finds herself surveying the possibility of a new kind of life.

She's out of the box!

The synagogue leader goes ballistic. No doubt, in his outrage he speaks for many. How dare Jesus work on the Sabbath? Why, even God does not work on the Sabbath! Such are the rules. He tells Jesus such healing work should not be done on the Sabbath. After all, there are six other days in the week when the woman might come to the synagogue and seek healing.

The remark staggers me. I wonder how many times this woman had done just that. Does the synagogue leader care how hard it must be for her to scrape together a living or make her way to the synagogue? Could he begin to imagine a scene in which he might have gone to the woman to help her?

Jesus cuts him no slack. He exposes the hypocrisy of the synagogue leader's assumptions and actions. As Jesus puts it, everyone finds a way to do needful work on the Sabbath. For example, people are allowed to untie and lead a donkey or ox to water. As for the woman, she "is a child of Abraham, even as you say" (v. 16, version mine). Surely she deserves no less consideration.

In effect, Jesus says, "When God must choose between the rules and people, God goes with people." The leader has no ready response, mostly because there is none. God is for people, period! The common folk rejoice to hear the words of Jesus. The woman, who does not fit into the world of the synagogue leader, fits very well in God's world.

For those with ears to hear, that's good news.

All of which brings me back to boxes. The story raises some box-related questions with which we must deal.

First, have I been trying to force God into a box? That is, have I been trying to force God to play by what I regard as "the rules"? Such rules spring from our birth culture, traditions, and even personal preferences. Ask yourself, "Have I been saying to God, 'I know what you will and will not do, what you can and cannot do, who you can love and who you must despise, who you can save or heal and who is beyond your reach. I know the rules you have to play by, God.'"

Are you trying to stuff God into a box?

Second, have I been trying to force others into a box? Have I looked at them and said, "I know where you belong, what is possible for you, and how you fit in with God and others. I'm going to put you in your place and keep you there."

Third, have I been living in a box? Am I saying to God, "I know where I fit into the world, society, church, and family. I know what I am. I'm in this box, and I have to stay there. It's really not so bad—not good, but it could be worse. I'm in my box, and not even God can get me out."

My guess is that all of us play with boxes when it comes to God, others, and even ourselves.

There's a better way, and it starts when you and I catch a glimpse of the Jesus who tears open boxes. Christ continues to rip apart the boxes in which we live or place others. What might happen in our lives, the life of the congregation, or the life of the larger world if we joined Christ in such work?

Perhaps a prayer will help us get started.

Lord, show us the boxes into which we try to put other humans. Help us name each box. Break our hearts even as we do so. Help us repent of ever having placed a fellow human in a box.

Help us see and name the boxes into which others have placed us or into which we've placed ourselves. Grant that we may resolve, with your help, to break free of our boxes and never be boxed in again. Lead us, Lord, to become people who liberate others from boxes as well. In the name of the Father, Son, and Holy Spirit, amen.

30

A Meditation: Mustard Seeds and Yeast

Luke 13:18-21

Jesus teaches us to pray that God's will be done on earth as it is in heaven. Certainly that's our desire, even though we're unsure what that might look like in a world filled with people, animals, weather, tectonic plates, viruses, plants, and all the other stuff of creation. We can hardly help asking just how such a thing might come to pass.

There's no lack of people who like to try to answer the question for us.

Just the other day I watched a television preacher who said the surest way to advance God's kingdom on earth was to make a contribution to his organization and receive his latest "free" book. Skipping over a few channels, I encountered another minister with a different take on the matter. He argued that God's kingdom would start to come on earth if we elected candidates from a certain political party.

Jesus offers a different perspective. Rather than look to the worlds of commerce or politics, he turns instead to the metaphors of a garden and a bakery.

In a garden, small seeds grow into mature plants, which in turn provide food plus seeds for the subsequent planting season. A bread baker knows that a tiny amount of yeast may transform the look, feel, and taste of an entire pan of bread dough. Jesus says the kingdom of God works like seeds and yeast.

Could it be that small actions done in accordance with God's will matter beyond themselves? Jesus believes so, and since you and I follow him, I suppose we ought to try to believe it as well.

A young woman of my acquaintance decided to try to help people in Haiti recover from the effects of an earthquake. She was a high school student at the time. What difference could a high school student make?

It turns out, quite a bit. She went to Haiti and worked directly to help people get the food and shelter they needed. When she returned to her hometown, she founded a nonprofit that enlists young people to continue the work. Adults noticed and joined as well. After a few years, my friend moved on to other ministry endeavors, but the nonprofit continues to meet real needs in Haiti. My friend's relatively small actions turned out to have long-term, ever-widening results.

Let's go spread some mustard seeds, stir some yeast into a vat of dough, speak a word on behalf of the least of these, and do whatever good we can. And let's take hope and joy in doing so. As it turns out, that's how the kingdom of God works.

31

Let's Talk about the Narrow Gate

Luke 13:22–14:35

Two Christian friends of long standing sat at a table with me in a Mexican restaurant. Over chips, salsa, and artery-clogging burritos, we ran through old debates, ending with the one to which we always returned.

"Mike," my friend said, "let's talk about the narrow gate. I think you're too generous when it comes to the question of who's in and who's out with God when all is said and done. Jesus talked about a narrow gate, a narrow door, and he warned that very few would make it through that gate."

Sometimes, if you're like me, you wonder if it's really worth the energy to go on discussing a given matter, even with a good friend. Still, I could not resist trying one more time.

"Well, as far as I can tell, that's not quite the point Jesus made."

The conversation took off. We did not settle the matter that day, and I doubt we ever will. My friend is committed to a viewpoint that essentially maintains one must confess Jesus as Lord in a certain way, be baptized in a particular manner, and live a lifestyle often (though inaccurately) described as Victorian.

Jesus, I think, takes a different approach.

One day someone asks him, "Lord, will only a few be saved?" (13:23). I think it's obvious that the questioner probably considers himself to be among the few and is looking for confirmation from Jesus. If so, Jesus disappoints him. Luke records a series of events and sayings in which Jesus describes those who will find and enter through the narrow door.

Jesus insists that all must strive to find and enter by the narrow door. Pay attention to the verb translated "strive" (v. 24). That's an important clue to what Jesus has in mind. Much to the dismay of the Protestant mindset,

Jesus insists that people have to work at finding and going through the narrow door!

In the verses that follow, he expands on the matter. Note that he nowhere points to a set of beliefs, written confessions of faith, modes of baptism, theories related to the Lord's Supper, or anything similar. He does not even hold out much hope for those who simply socialize with him while he goes about his business. In fact, he suggests that those who rely on such things may find themselves on the wrong side of the narrow door when all is said and done. Those whom the people of God believe are excluded from the Messianic feast will be included, though they come from all walks of life and from all over the world.

If the narrow gate has little or nothing to do with doctrine, church ordinances, bloodlines, and such, just what does Jesus have in mind?

If we pay attention to what Jesus does, we'll find some answers. Start with an occasion (14:1ff) when Jesus is on his way to eat a meal on the Sabbath with a leader from among the Pharisees. Along the way, he encounters a sick man.

Turning to the lawyers and Pharisees who are accompanying him, he asks whether it is lawful to cure people on the Sabbath. Both he and they know the approved answer to be no. Jesus then cures the man and twits his religious company, reminding them that they do not let the Sabbath get in the way of caring for one of their children or even an ox.

What are we to do if we hope to find and enter through the narrow door and so start to live the Jesus kind of life now and forever? We start by learning to spot human need, stripping away any religious scruples that make us hesitate to address the need, and doing all we can to help. When we make this our lifestyle, we're well on our way.

When they arrive at the dinner, Jesus notices seating patterns. The various guests select the seats of honor nearest the host. No one competes for the seats at the far end of the dining area! Social competition is in, and humility is out—even at a meal whose guests are highly religious. Jesus counsels them to reverse their goals, practice humility, and take the least of the positions. Such humility may prove an end in itself, or it may open the way for the host to invite a guest to move up.

How are we to find and enter through the narrow door and so start to live the Jesus kind of life now and forever? According to Jesus, the practice of humility is a key requirement.

Jesus proves to be a challenging lunch guest. He goes on to tell his host he ought to revise his thinking and his guest list. Instead of inviting relatives, friends, and important folk who may repay him in some way, he instead should invite those who cannot repay him. The list Jesus provides is daunting in any era: "the poor, the crippled, the lame, and the blind" (14:13).

I wonder whom Jesus might include on such a list in our era. Surely the poor, sick, blind, and disabled would remain on the list. I suspect he would also provide examples from the long list of people who live on the fringe of "acceptable" society in our day. People with HIV, people caught in multiple-generation poverty, immigrants of all kinds, and other such people come to my mind.

How are we to find and enter through the narrow door and so start to live the Jesus kind of life now and forever? If Jesus is to be believed, the practice of hospitality to those who can offer little or nothing in return is required.

Jesus is on a roll, and soon he launches into a parable. He tells of someone who gives a great dinner only to find that all the important and righteous people invited send regrets and excuses. The excuses are rooted in the routines of their daily lives.

The host, angered, sends his servants out to find and bring others to the banquet: "the poor, the crippled, the blind, and the lame" (v. 21). Even so, there's room remaining at the table, so the owner sends out the servants to find and bring to the meal everyone else possible. Those who first were invited but declined to come at the appointed time are left out.

What does Jesus have in mind? At the very least, he warns us against presumption, against the notion that we can trifle with God's invitation to enter into the Jesus kind of life, even if the invitation comes to us while we are busy with our current lives. Those who are unencumbered with stuff, possessions, making money, and the like—those who have need and know it—might just be closer to entering God's kingdom than they (or we) realize.

How are we to find and enter through the narrow door and so start to live the Jesus kind of life now and forever? Jesus insists that a key element involves being always ready to hear and accept God's invitation to do something in the world with God the moment God invites us to do so.

Sometime after the banquet, Jesus is traveling, and large crowds move along with him. They, perhaps, like to think that doing so means they're with Jesus.

If so, Jesus' words in 14:25-35 no doubt give them pause. He urges them to count the cost of following him, and he lays out the cost in hyperbolic images. Those who follow him must put doing so ahead of all other commitments, even those society or religion count as most sacred. Given that this is so, it's no wonder that Jesus goes on to say, "none of you can become my disciple if you do not give up all your possessions" (v. 33). In other words, we must give up anything that will cause us to hesitate to listen to Jesus, go with Jesus, emulate what Jesus does, or do as Jesus instructs.

While I lived in Memphis, I met an elderly black man who had been active in the Civil Rights Movement. One day he said to me, "We had to count the cost before we marched with Martin Luther King. It was not theoretical. Marching could cost us our jobs, such as they were. Marching could lead to someone shooting at us or our families, tossing a stick of dynamite through the window one night, or kidnapping and killing us. No sir, there was nothing theoretical about what it cost to go with Martin, just like there's nothing theoretical about what it costs to go with Jesus."

As I listened to him, Jesus' warning about counting the cost of following him came alive for me.

Here's what I've come to know. We're most likely to find and enter into the Jesus kind of life through the narrow door when we practice helping those in need, humility, radical hospitality, ready response to each opportunity for ministry God offers, and laying all we hold dear on the line.

The road to such a narrow door starts here, now, today.

Who will take it?

32

Come Home

Luke 15:1-32

Once when the scribes and Pharisees grumbled about how Jesus welcomed sinners, Jesus told three parables.

The first is about a shepherd who went to extraordinary lengths to find a single lost sheep and return it to the fold. The second speaks of a woman with ten silver coins. She lost one of them and would not rest until she found it. When each found what had been lost, the shepherd and the woman called together friends and neighbors to rejoice with them.

Both parables depict people driven by a single purpose that supersedes all other considerations. In the third parable, Jesus turns attention to the overriding hope of God.

The story goes like this: Two sons lived with their father on the family farm. Contrary to all the laws and customs of the day, the younger son asked his father to give him his inheritance, and without regard for those same laws and customs, the father did so.

The younger son went to a far country, blew his inheritance, and wound up taking a job on a farm and doing work even a slave was not asked to do back on his father's farm. At last the young man came to his senses, got up, and started home. Along the way, he composed a speech of repentance in hope of being allowed to return to the farm as a servant.

His father, though, had never ceased to think of him and watch for his return. When he saw his son trudging toward home, the father cast aside all propriety, ran to him, embraced him, shushed his apology, and declared him his child. The father even threw a party to celebrate his son's return.

The older son, who had never understood what his father saw in his younger brother, had stayed on the farm in accordance with law and tradition. When a farm hand came to summon him to the party, he grew angry and refused to attend.

His father—who seemingly had little if any personal need to maintain his honor—went to the older son. He urged him to enter the house and enjoy the party. The older son erupted in anger, called his younger brother worthless, and accused his father of playing favorites.

His father gently reminded him that he, the older son, now owned everything the father owned. The younger son had nothing except the love and grace of his father and the potential love and grace of his brother. Wouldn't the older son relent, recognize the younger son as his brother, enter the father's house, and join the party?

Now, that's quite a story. The longer I live with it, the more I find myself thinking about the brothers.

They seem so different from one another. One lives in accordance with cultural expectations while the other breaks all the rules.

As it turns out, though, they are very much alike. They share a similar attitude toward their father. Both wish he would get out of the way so that each of them could run his own life his own way. Both accept their portion of the inheritance when it is offered. One rebels openly. The other tries to remake his father and the farm in his own image. Neither loves and trusts the father.

Each is "lost." Lost in worldviews manufactured by their malformed spirituality; lost to one another; lost to any sense of how vital the father is to them and their well-being; lost to any awareness of how deeply their father loves each of them; lost to their shared need for humility and forgiveness.

Both need to come to their senses. The younger son's need is easy for us to see. His behavior and its consequences send the message loud and clear. Even when he wakes up and realizes he needs to go home to his father, he comprehends only his own brokenness. He cannot yet begin to fathom the restorative depths of his father's love.

It's harder for us to see the older son's need. He keeps up appearances, meets normal expectations, and does not break openly with his father until late in the story. Yet he fools himself about himself, for he desires to dominate his father and set the agenda for the farm. He is lost and does not know it.

Both need to come home to their father. Each son needs to break his established view of himself, his father, and the world. Both need to repent, rise, and make their way to their father. Each needs to find and embrace humility and seek forgiveness. One does. The other does not, at least not within the confines of the story.

I think a great deal about the two sons, and I often ask myself which one I most resemble.

The longer I live with the story, the more amazed I am by the father. He gives away the farm, gifting both his sons with their desired inheritance. The action runs contrary to the practice of the day and common sense. It would have scandalized the neighbors, who would have thought the father a fool without honor and the boys lawbreakers. The father commits an act of self-forgetful love and humility. He is a father who loves so deeply that he breaks all the rules regarding a father's honor.

The father allows each son freedom to choose his own way. He does so even though each son breaks the father's heart because of poor decisions and lack of love for one another.

I am struck by how he watches, ever hopeful, for their return. We are familiar with the image of the father watching the road for the openly prodigal son's return. I think he watched as well for the return of the older son. I see the father watching at the end of each workday for his older son to return from the fields and embrace him as his father. The days go by, and neither son shows up. Still, the father watches and waits.

Most of all I'm struck by how he treats each of his sons as the story winds down. He speaks no word of direct or indirect reproach to the prodigal son. The father rejects the boy's attempt to manage his return by relinquishing his birthright. Instead, the father declares him his son, throws a party to celebrate his return, and starts to reintegrate him into the life of the family.

As for the older son, the father goes outside rather than demanding his angry son come to him. He listens to his son's speech. The father gently corrects his son on two counts. First, despite his desire to sever all ties with his younger brother, they remain siblings. Second, the reinstatement of the younger brother does not diminish the older son's inheritance in any way. And in spite of all the older brother has said and done, the father invites him to come to his senses, come inside the home of his father, and join the party.

The longer I live with the story, the more I find myself asking one question: What will I do with this kind of God? The parable suggests some answers.

I can run and keep on running from this kind of God. Perhaps I don't feel comfortable with everyone that God includes in the family. Maybe I want to feel in charge of my life and answerable to no one. Who knows? All

I know is that sometimes I've chosen to run. The strategy has never worked out well, but I've tried it.

I might choose to stay, keep up appearances, and try to force God to see and do things my way. If I were a gambler, I would bet that's what most of us do. We claim God's resources as our own and use them toward our own ends. We attempt to manage God, tell God whom God can love and whom God can welcome into the Body of Christ and treat as family. I can play the part of the older brother. You can, too.

A third option seems best to me: I can come to my senses, come home to the God who loves me, experience God's welcome, and in turn embrace all the others God welcomes to God's family. I can join the party. Who knows? I might even wind up enjoying it!

I think you might, too.

33

Lessons from a Bad Man

Luke 16:1–18

When I became the pastor of a small church in Nashville, Tennessee, soon after graduating from seminary, a retired businessman gave a book to me and urged me to read it.

"This book," he said, "changed my life when I was a young man. The stories in it inspired me to try to do the right thing, work hard, and make some difference in the world."

The book was a collection of brief stories about people who overcame adversity and went on to success of some kind. Certainly, the book bore traces of heavy use: a worn cover, dog-eared pages, a cracked spine, and notes scribbled in the margins.

I thumbed through the book recently. (Yes, I kept it all these years. I'm a little sentimental about the older friend who gave it to me.) As I skimmed the stories, something struck me: each was the story of a fundamentally good person who faced severe challenges, overcame them, and went on to do good things.

Stories of fundamentally good people . . . those are the stories we tend to read and tell. But is it possible to learn good things from the lives of dishonorable people?

Jesus thought so. His Parable of the Dishonest Business Manager is a case in point.

The brief tale goes like this: A rich man learned that his business manager had mismanaged his accounts and lined his own pockets. The business manager heard his boss was about to fire him, and he took action to protect his future. He called in many of those who owed his employer large sums of money, offered them a chance to settle their debts at an enormous discount, closed the deals, and so put the debtors in his debt.

Can you imagine those listening to Jesus tell the story? How do you think they expected it to end? I suspect they thought the story would end with the man's employer catching him, firing him, and sending him off to prison. After all, surely Jesus was telling a morality story, a tale warning against a life of deception and theft, something that would drive home a point, perhaps something as simple as "Crime doesn't pay."

Instead, Jesus surprised them by praising the villain for his shrewdness, by which Jesus specifically meant the man's focus on finding ways to make friends for himself.

Personally, I wish Jesus had chosen another story, one more like those in the book my elderly friend gave me so long ago.

But I get the Lord's point, I think. Wouldn't it be wise for Christians to spend more time making friends rather than enemies in the world?

In Jesus' time, substantial segments of the Jewish population thought of much of the world as an enemy to be avoided or overcome. I'm afraid many of us have fallen into a similar pattern of thought and behavior. Do you doubt me? Think. How many times have you read or heard a Christian speak of those of another religion, those who differ with them about politics and social issues, and even other kinds of Christians as enemies? When we start to pay attention and actually notice such behavior, we're amazed at its scope.

Jesus called his people to take a different approach to others: find points of common concern and need, address such matters in a way that is helpful to others, and thus build positive relationships.

Jesus envisioned a world in which many outside the Christian faith might come to say, "That Christian is a friend to me" or "The church helps people."

How about it? Are you ready to learn something valuable from the story of a dishonorable person? I hope so. Jesus thought it was important.

And he was right.

34

The Lazarus Challenge

Luke 16:19–31

Sooner or later, a sensitive person is driven to ask a pointed question: "Why do so many people go without food, medical care, or even friends in a world where so many religious people live?"

A second question soon follows: "Is it supposed to be this way?"

Jesus responded to such questions by telling a parable about a rich man and a poor man. The rich man goes about his daily life without regard for a poor, sick man who lies outside the gates to his home. Lazarus, the poor man, is too weak to fend off street dogs that lick his sores.

Eventually, both men die. Lazarus goes to "the bosom of Abraham" while the rich man awakens in a hellish place of thirst and torment.

Startled by such a reversal, the rich man looks up, sees Lazarus resting under the protection of Abraham, and complains. He implores Abraham to send Lazarus to quench his thirst. When Abraham refuses, the rich man asks him to send Lazarus to the rich man's brothers to warn them to mend their ways. Again Abraham refuses, reminding the rich man that Moses and the prophets commanded all God's people to care for the poor. As Abraham puts it, if God's folk will not listen to Moses and the prophets, they will not pay attention even to one who returns from the dead.

The story, to my mind, lays down four challenges.

The first challenge is to *choose to see the least of these in the course of our daily lives.* The rich man had a particular, well-established way of looking at the world. His routines consumed each day's time and energies.

As do most of ours.

The rich man felt that he knew who he needed to see on a given day: immediate family, business partners, the movers and shakers of his world.

As do most of us.

Lazarus, to be honest, had a place in the rich man's world—the place of the "invisible one," the person the rich man would never notice even though Lazarus lay at his gate.

Jesus challenges us to learn to see, notice, and focus on those in need in the course of our daily lives. It's not easy, and certainly it's not always comfortable, but it's our Jesus-initiated calling.

The second challenge is to *choose to care*. Given his tone throughout the parable, I suspect the rich man thought, "Why should I care about Lazarus or anyone like him?"

Quite a few folks, including Christians, exhibit such a mindset. In my experience, their callousness is driven by one or more factors.

Bad theology often plays a role. The popular theology of Jesus' day held that a person such as Lazarus must be suffering because of sin, whether his own or the sin of his parents. The rich man might have thought he need not or should not care for someone whose poor choices or outright sin landed him in dire circumstances.

Perhaps he thought Lazarus's own family should have taken care of him. He may have thought the "safety net" administered by the temple and some synagogues ought to get the job done.

I wonder if he did not help because deep inside he did not feel securely rich. Did he fear the proverbial wolf at the door, believe he had little margin, and so could not risk generosity?

Maybe something deeper and darker was in play. Had the rich man's heart hardened over the years, so that he no longer had the capacity to care about Lazarus or people like him? I rather think this likely, since even in death he reserved his concern for his own needs and his immediate family.

Here's the rub: we are more nearly like the rich man than we care to admit. Compassion fatigue and compassion restriction are real. Prejudice, bad theology, insecurity, and hard hearts combine to shut down our capacity to care for the least of these.

Jesus calls us to choose to become people who want to see and help those in need.

The third challenge is to *make caring personal*. Even if the rich man had noticed Lazarus, he might have been afraid to get involved in a personal way. Who has not held back from involvement because we were afraid of possible effects on our family, time, reputation, and finances?

In the rich man's case, though, I think the real challenge was to break through all his assumptions and see that Lazarus was as much his family as were his own biological brothers. Lazarus was his particular opportunity, a person at his gate with a name, history, and need. In Lazarus, the rich man had a chance to care personally for someone in deep need, and to do so even if there was a good chance that person would die anyway.

Jesus challenges all who would claim his name to take our seeing and our caring and give it personal expression.

The fourth challenge is to *act*. The rich man did not act to help Lazarus. Both Lazarus and he paid a price. One died in misery, and the other died and found himself in exile from God.

The rich man never learned, never came to grips with his failure.

But we can. As the old-time preachers used to say, we can change our "want to" into "will do."

How might we do so?

The church can help you. Volunteer to serve in your congregation and in one or two of the many ministries we partner with. Ask a minister or volunteer coordinator to sit down with you to help you find a ministry or service area that matches your skills and interests. Or just say, "Put me somewhere." We can help you take up the challenge Jesus issued.

Make intentional gifts of money so that someone in need has a place to sleep, clothing, food, or medical care. One of our mission partners works extensively in such ways. In a given year, about five to ten dollars can provide a blanket or a coat or three boxes of food for a refugee family. Sixty dollars or so can usually provide a month's worth of emergency shelter in many parts of the world. One hundred and thirty-five to two hundred dollars can provide a doctor or skilled nurse for an entire month in many locations around the world.

My point is this: your time, skills, and money—the very stuff of your life—can be directed toward helping the least of these get the minimum help they need to live. You and I can do so in the name of Jesus, knowing Jesus expects nothing less.

Be careful not to underestimate how difficult such a change in perspective, feelings, and action may prove. Taken together, they represent a sea change in the way we spend our lives.

Such changes are precisely what God wants for each of us, and God stands ready to empower us as we live into such lives.

Let's go together and look to see who is lying outside our gate.

35

Words for Disciples in the Making

Luke 17:1–10

Most of us make use of guidelines.

For example, I like a particular set of guidelines related to making statements. The guidelines have been attributed to quite a range of people, including Socrates and Buddha, but regardless of their origin, I find them useful in the world of Facebook, Twitter, and other social media. Before posting anything, I try to remember to ask myself, "Is it true, is it kind, and is it necessary?"

I'm sure you have sets of guidelines you turn to as well.

In Luke 17:1-10, Jesus provides some guidelines to his disciples in the making. The guidelines remain challenging and useful as we strive to build a Christian community.

The first guideline goes like this: *don't put stumbling blocks to trusting God in the way of others.* Jesus, realist that he is, admits that all of us encounter such stumbling blocks. He insists, though, that his disciples must guard against being the kind of folk who produce and place stumbling blocks in the way of others.

I wonder if we give much thought to how our words, expectations, and deeds might hinder others from choosing to trust God. I suspect we need to ramp up our efforts.

Do you think people have ever turned away from God because of a Christian they know? I do. I deal with such matters on an ongoing basis. I know individuals who simply find it impossible to believe in God because of their experience with one or more of us.

I think of a middle-aged woman who experienced more than a decade of mental and physical abuse from her churchgoing husband. Her husband often quoted Scripture to justify his actions. Is it any wonder she finds it hard to trust God or Christians?

Then there's a Jewish friend of mine who admires Jesus but cannot take the Christian faith seriously because of the number of Christian bigots he encounters at work, at school, and in politics.

In these and other situations, the problem lies not with God or the victims. The professed followers of Jesus are the problem.

It seems to me that Jesus calls us to surrender all excuses, examine ourselves closely, and turn from any words, attitudes, and actions that might cause others to doubt God's love.

Second, Jesus insists his followers *work with one another to foster a community of honesty and ready forgiveness.* Confronted with such an expectation, the apostles exclaim, "Increase our faith!" (v. 5).

Why are they so taken aback? Put bluntly, they cannot envision learning to trust God and one another enough to build and inhabit such a community. Let's not kid ourselves about the downside of human nature. Left to our own devices, we tend to look after our perceived self-interests. We find it difficult to believe we can trust others enough to live together in community while practicing directness, confession, and forgiveness.

Jesus demands that we not settle for building community around typical kinds of self-interest. He calls us to imagine and work toward the kind of Christian community in which we do not fear one another but instead live by faith for one another.

The challenge of building such a community leads to the third guideline: *the faith we already have is enough to empower building a strong community of faith.*

When the apostles plead for increased faith, Jesus responds that even the tiniest bit is enough to do what needs doing and more. They find this hard to believe. We do, too.

The trick is to start and go on trying to build the kind of community Jesus envisions. In my experience, faith deepens and matures in the context of action. Stick with the dream, accept the pain of failures, take some joy at each success, and stay on task. When we do so, we soon are forced to admit our limits and lean more fully on God. Hard-earned humility fuels faith.

The fourth guideline is to *embrace the life of a servant.* A servant tends to his or her assigned task, regardless of the hour of the day, exhaustion, or the mood of other workers. Such servants strengthen community.

Christian servanthood is a mindset wed to practice. Servants seldom get noticed, and at their best they do not seek attention. They simply do whatever needs doing to tend to the well-being of the community of faith. Their actions and attitude set the tone of the community's life. The surest way to surprise a servant is to thank them. Almost always, the servant's first thought is, "I was only doing what I ought to have done."

As congregations in the twenty-first century try to find their way through cultural shifts, political upheavals, generational transitions, and economic storms, Jesus' guidelines chart our best path forward. Let's go where they lead us.

36

Jesus and the Lepers

Luke 17:11-19

I've been thinking about the story of Jesus and the lepers, and here's some of what has come to me.

Jesus and his followers are on the way to Jerusalem through a kind of no-man's land nestled between Samaria and Galilee. By this point in Luke's Gospel, Jesus has set his sights on getting to Jerusalem and bringing his mission to a conclusion. He has much on his mind.

As he approaches a village, no doubt with the intention of moving through and continuing on his way, ten lepers approach him.

How will Jesus respond? He has important things to do. Few would blame him for ignoring the lepers and moving on.

I rather doubt the lepers would fault him. They seem to buy into the prevailing perspective on their plight, the religion-fueled viewpoint which teaches they somehow deserve to be inflicted with their fatal disease. Deep in their hearts, they're convinced that their sin or the sin of some forebearer brought the wrath of God upon them in this way.

As a result, they play by the rules of the day. They keep a prescribed distance between them and others, form a little band for protection and support, and live outside the village. They feel shamed by their disease, accept exile from society, and expect to die alone except for the company of fellow lepers.

The lepers interact with Jesus in the only way permitted them: they keep their distance and cry out for mercy. "Jesus, Master, have mercy on us" (v. 13).

I don't know what they hope or expect might happen. If they have heard of the healing ministry of Jesus, perhaps they dare hope he might heal them. At the very least, he might give them a bit of money or some food.

I do know one thing. Unlike many whom Jesus encounters, the lepers know they need mercy. They have nothing in the way of family, heritage, wealth, profession, or future prospects left.

They call out to Jesus, and Jesus pays attention and exercises mercy. He says, "Go and show yourselves to the priests" (v. 14).

Such is the language of the law of the land. If by some unthinkable chance a leper should be healed, the leper must go and be examined by the priests. Only when the priests certify that the leper is well might the person return to family, work, worship, and friends—return to life, as it were.

When Jesus tells them to go, they are still lepers. He does not heal them on the spot but only tells them to start moving. On the way, they notice they are healed.

Slow down and pay attention: the lepers are healed as they move along in response to Jesus. I'm struck by the lack of preliminaries. They call out for mercy, Jesus tells them to go to the priests, they start on the way in obedience to Jesus, and healing comes to them.

As far as I can determine, Jesus lays no requirement on the lepers other than to start walking in the direction he tells them take.

That's grace in action. The theology that considers illness divine punishment for sin is deeply flawed, but Jesus does not demand that the lepers reject it in order to be healed. He does not require them to join his band or buck the system that marginalizes and excludes them.

All Jesus does is break them out of stasis, out of their holding pattern, and set them on a journey marked by new hope, which might morph into trust in God when all is said and done.

Often I wish we could learn to practice Jesus' self-restraint in our dealings with others. Too often, what we offer is grace with numerous conditions attached, stipulations that require the one receiving grace to meet our expectations or needs in some way.

The ways in which we do so range from the trivial to the tragic. I've known Christians who insisted one had to reject certain forms of dress, music, worship, and hairstyle in order to be welcomed into the church. On more than one occasion, I've listened as otherwise sensible Christians have told me one could not be a Christian and belong to a particular political party. We, more than we might care to admit, believe grace ought to transform others into people who agree with and act like us.

Jesus, in contrast, does not even ask to be thanked. Oh, mind you, he takes joy in the gratitude of the one healed man who comes back to thank him. The man happens to be a Samaritan, the last person the Jewish followers of Jesus would expect to express gratitude in this way. Jesus praises the Samaritan, tells him his faith has healed him, and sends him along.

But Jesus does not revoke the healing of the other nine former lepers. Instead, he allows them to live into the new lives he freely gives them. Apparently, Jesus does not fear to turn grace loose in the world. Rather than seek to control how such grace might play out, he keeps moving toward Jerusalem, where—when all is said and done—he will make such grace available to all.

Frankly, the tale makes me wonder if we've really gotten hold of this grace thing. Are you and I willing to try to accept and practice a grace that does not set preconditions and try to control outcomes? Can we learn to live with and take joy in God's wild grace?

Sometimes I think if ever we did so, we might just surprise Jesus at least as much as did the Samaritan who returned to give thanks.

37

The Kingdom of God Is Now

Luke 17:20-37

Do you know where many pastors invest much of their time?

Go ahead. Make a mental list of possible answers. What are you putting on the list? Study, writing sermons, visiting the sick, evangelism, church administration, killing time between Sundays (that one's a joke!)?

Many of the pastors I know spend a great deal of time inviting people to lay aside assumptions and see God, themselves, others, and life in a new way.

To be honest, it's hard work. We're attached to our assumptions, even when we scarcely realize they exist. If we are not careful, or if someone does not help us recognize them, we are apt to live in service to largely unexamined assumptions.

Such was the case with the Pharisees and the disciples regarding the question of when they should expect the kingdom of God to arrive. They anticipated a future event and wanted to know the signs that would foreshadow it.

Cut them some slack. Their perspective was deeply rooted in the religious culture. My guess is that if you or I had interviewed one hundred first-century Jewish people in Palestine, nine out of ten would have thought of the kingdom of God as a future event.

In that one respect, they were much like many Christians in the United States. We've been reared in a religious culture fascinated by speculation about the "end time" and the signs of those times.

For the most part, our fixation stems from a theological system called premillennial dispensationalism. Such an approach to the Scriptures traces back to the work of an Englishman named John Darby. In the US,

C. I. Scofield and his reference Bible have spread the theological scheme to large segments of American Christianity. One result is a tendency on the part of many of us to look for the kingdom of God to arrive at some future date.

Pay attention: Jesus rejected the assumption. He insisted, "in fact, the kingdom of God is among you" (v. 21).

If we took Jesus seriously, large segments of the Christian publishing and movie industries would collapse. Instead of shelling out money to buy the latest book about the end of the world, we would reframe our lives around a new question: "How can I discern the kingdom of God right now in the life of the world and in my life?"

Jesus taught that the kingdom of God is already here and operative. He warned his first disciples (and us) to stop looking for end-time signs in culture, economics, politics, religion, or even the weather. Drawing on stories from the Hebrew Scriptures, Jesus reminded his listeners that life was going on as usual in the days of Noah and Lot. Most folk in those days did not realize God was at work in the midst of it all.

So it would prove to be with Jesus. He would move among people, no doubt stirring up debate and opposition, but in the end he would suffer and die and most—including his disciples—would believe his story ended there.

The resurrection would surprise everyone. It would create a world in which two people sharing a bed or a task might make different decisions that either aligned or misaligned them with God's ongoing work in the world. Only those who turned loose of what they had and risked throwing in their lot with God would find real life.

I know all of this sounds mysterious, but it makes a drastic difference in how we live.

If we're looking for the world to end, and if we tend to think the world will only get worse until the end, we're not overly motivated to address poverty, war, illness, political imprisonment, or anything else on Jesus' agenda (see Luke 4). On the other hand, if we see God at work everywhere in the world in the present moment and Christ in each person—well, that changes things. I find it hard to walk away and leave the Christ we see in others unfairly jailed, shut out of economic opportunity, victimized by careless warfare, or left to cope alone with illness.

When we see and admit that the kingdom of God is already among us, we're more apt to take on kingdom tasks now.

And that's precisely what Jesus had in mind!

38

Questions I Ask Myself

Luke 18:1-17

Luke tells stories to prompt us to reflect on our life with Christ. Take for example the three stories found in Luke 18:1-17. They pose three questions I'm trying to learn to ask myself on a frequent basis.

How do I see God? In the parable, a widow pesters an unjust judge until she wears him down and he grants her justice. The judge is not admirable. In fact, it's clear he normally abuses his power and caters to the needs of the powerful. We smile as his resistance slowly erodes under the widow's relentless assault.

Our problem is that we sometimes see God as a distant deity whose attention is hard to get. We may wonder how God could possibly have time enough to care about us. Perhaps we envision God as a kind of Big Bang God, who launched creation but then stepped out of the picture. Too many of us, I think, confuse God with an adult authority figure from our past who was cold and distant, the kind of adult who noticed us only when we made a lot of noise.

How we see God determines how we approach God. Each day I try to remember that Jesus said God is not like the unjust judge. God, instead, is attentive to us, hears our prayers, and is always at work in our lives. When I buy into Jesus' way of seeing God, prayer becomes an ongoing conversation with a trusted Lord.

The Parable of the Pharisee and the Tax Collector generates a second question: *How do I see myself?* Jesus draws a sharp contrast between the tax collector and the Pharisee. The first builds his life on the basis of his ongoing need for God's mercy, the second on his list of well-defined accomplishments. The tax collector petitions God for mercy, and the Pharisee sends God a bill for his services.

I would like to be able to say that I have much in common with the tax collector. The truth of the matter is that I've had to struggle against a tendency to measure myself by achievable standards. That's the American way, after all. When I let down my guard, I can easily fall into the trap of setting lifestyle and worship goals I can meet, doing so, patting myself on the back, and saying to God, "Look at me and what I've done. Aren't you proud?"

The Pharisee's pride left untouched aspects of his life of which I suspect he was unaware. If he was typical of the time, he no doubt regarded Gentiles and women as second-class humans and acted accordingly. He clearly felt it was right to denigrate those he regarded as sinners. My hunch is that he thought of himself as one of God's guardians, as someone who had earned the right to determine who was worthy to enter the synagogue or temple.

On my bad days, I'm such a person, but deep inside I want to be something else. Don't you?

That's why I go on asking how I see myself. How I see myself affects how I perceive God and others. The more I see myself as someone in need of mercy, the more I find myself able to receive and give mercy.

Is there still a bit of the child in me? This third question arises from the story of the children, the disciples, and Jesus.

People start bringing their children to Jesus in hopes that he will heal or bless them by his touch. The disciples, who share their culture's general view that children are somehow less important than adults, attempt to block the way. The disciples come across as people filled with their own importance, an inflated self-perception fueled perhaps by their need to be seen as the handlers of Jesus and by a misplaced confidence in their knowledge of what matters to Jesus.

Jesus intervenes and clears the way for the children to come to him. To the astonishment of the disciples, he says the children know more than they do about how to interact with God. He insists they must learn from children. I don't think the disciples liked the idea.

When I first began to think about the kind of person I wanted to become, I admit that becoming childlike was not on my list of goals. I like children (though I did not enjoy being one), but I also know children have much to learn about themselves, others, and God.

"Much to learn"—that's the key. Ideally, to be childlike is to know one has much to learn and to be open to doing so. Jesus calls us to become such people.

So I ask myself, is there still a bit of the child in me? Am I still open to what God and others might teach me? When is the last time I changed my mind as a result of new information or insight? Am I alive or am I already fossilized? What does the evidence suggest?

How do I see God? How do I see myself? Is there still a bit of the child in me? Three questions a day help me live more nearly aware of the kingdom of God. Take them, use them, and see for yourself the difference they make.

39

The Man with Everything

Luke 18:18-34

Some conversations muddle along and don't take us much of anywhere. Others, though, shake us up, reveal our values, help us understand ourselves and God better, and open up new possibilities.

Take the conversation between a rich ruler and Jesus as a case in point.

The ruler initiates the conversation. He asks Jesus what he must do to inherit eternal life. In response, Jesus points him to the commandments aimed at building healthy relationships and community.

When the ruler responds that he has kept all such commandments since his youth, Jesus does not dispute the claim. Instead, he redirects the conversation and tells the ruler he lacks one thing: "Sell all that you own and distribute the money to the poor, and you will have treasure in heaven; then come, follow me" (v. 22).

The ruler, whom Luke now tells us is very rich, is saddened by Jesus' answer. As far as we know from Luke's account, the ruler does not do as Jesus says.

The disciples of Jesus are astounded by the exchange. They, like most people in that time, believe riches are a sign of God's approval. Jesus, though, identifies material wealth as a grave danger to one's spiritual health.

The ruler is the real deal. Luke presents him as a person of no guile, pretense, or hypocrisy. He is what he says he is, a man who genuinely wants to please God. By any normal measure, he is a good person.

Still, he senses that something is missing. Though popular theology rates him as God-approved, he honestly does not feel at peace. He wonders if he is missing something vital. No doubt many try to assure him of his righteousness, but, to his credit, he seeks the input of Jesus.

It turns out that he's right: something is missing. He has failed to observe one key commandment: "I am the LORD your God . . . ; you shall have no other gods before me" (Ex 20:2-3). In practice (which is what matters most), the ruler trusts one thing more than God: his wealth. Such misplaced trust taints all his good works. He honors the community-building commandments only from a position of strength. He can afford to implement such commandments because doing so entails almost no risk to his place in society.

The ruler might as well pray something like this: "I give thanks and honor and worship to my wealth, which empowers me to live as if God is real." His uncertainty about his relationship with God stems from misplaced worship.

Jesus points the way out of his dilemma: turn loose of wealth, use it to help the poor, and take up the life of a pilgrim on the road with Jesus. The counsel sounds radical because it is.

Think of the ruler as someone addicted to wealth. Addicts cannot handle only a little of that to which they are addicted. Separation, abstinence, and new ways of self-definition are the only cures.

Luke tells us the ruler becomes sad. Again to his credit, he understands Jesus (which is more than we can say for the disciples!). He sees clearly the options before him, and the right choice is a hard one indeed. What will he do? Luke leaves the ruler's story open-ended.

Too often, we think his story has no direct connection to us. After all, most of us do not think of ourselves as rich. The truth, though, is that we are incredibly wealthy in comparison to most of the people who have lived over the course of human history. We face the same challenge as the rich ruler, for we are tempted to depend on our wealth rather than God. Like him, we find the first commandment the hardest of all the commandments to obey.

But we can choose to try.

Let's give it a go. Why not say something like this to Christ right now: "Yes, Jesus, I see your point. I confess I've not obeyed the first commandment and that my failure is the root cause of my insecurity before God. I want to walk away from that which keeps me from depending wholly on God. I will follow you and look to you to show me the way."

Yes, I know. This sounds impossible. All I can offer you is what Jesus said of impossible things, "What is impossible for mortals is possible for God."

40

Six Lessons for the Road

Luke 18:35–19:27

Jesus passes through Jericho. He is on his way to Jerusalem, where he will be arrested and die. Given the enormity of what is to come in Jerusalem, we might think Jesus would rush through Jericho.

Instead, he slows down to interact with two individuals and tell a parable. If we pay close attention, we soon discern that Jesus uses his time in Jericho to teach six important lessons for all those who would walk with him on this road.

First, get out of the way of those who want to interact with Jesus. The sad truth is that God's people often throw up barriers, or at least road blocks, to those who want to have a word with Jesus.

It's religious folk who try to shush the blind man and isolate Zacchaeus. No doubt they think their actions are justified in the eyes of God. After all, "everyone" knows illness is a punishment for sin, and "everyone" knows tax collectors are dishonest and traitors to their own people. Keep them in their place. Let them repent of their sin, and perhaps then they may be allowed to approach Jesus.

I wish I could say we were long past requiring people to jump through hoops before we believe they are ready for Jesus. I can't. Instead, often for what we regard as biblical or sound reasons, we treat them as if they should come to Jesus as we would have them to be rather than as they are.

Jesus takes a different approach. He hears the disabled man's call and insists the man be brought to him. He looks and sees Zacchaeus and speaks to him. Jesus makes it easy for people to come to him. Let's follow his lead.

Second, dare to come to Jesus from any starting point. The blind man certainly does so: he knows he wants to see. He comes to Jesus with his greatest felt need and shares that need with the Lord. Zacchaeus does the same. He comes to Jesus with his loneliness, isolation, and despair.

As it turns out, it's perfectly okay to come to Jesus from where you are.

I've seen people develop an interest in Jesus because of conviction of sin, friendships, intellectual curiosity, hearing a story or two, encountering Christians who live in countercultural ways, casual reading, a movie, and even (okay, only sometimes) a sermon.

Mark it down: there is no one starting place from which to seek and find Jesus. Start from where you are, and rejoice as others do the same.

Third, dare to go and see Jesus. The Zacchaeus story, in part, is the tale of a man who dares to go and see Jesus for himself. He does so in spite of genuine obstacles such as the size of the crowd, his small stature, the negative opinion most of the people have of him, and the real dangers he faces in such a crowd.

Sometimes I think the best invitation we might offer others is for them to go check out Jesus for themselves.

I suspect we need to do so as well. Too often, those of us who have spent our lives in church settle for the Jesus others describe to us or the Jesus we knew long years ago. We would do well to get up and go see Jesus for ourselves each day, even as we age and gain experience and so develop potential to see something in Jesus we could not discern earlier in life.

Fourth, dare to climb down and go home to dinner with Jesus. Zacchaeus comes down from the relative safety of the tree and goes home with Jesus. It's one thing to go and see Jesus; it's another to take him into our homes.

Home, by definition, is our sanctuary. It's the place where we feel safest and—at least in theory—are in charge. All of us have such sanctuaries. They range from our actual homes to our work, relationship networks, theological and behavioral structures, and imaginations.

When Zacchaeus takes Jesus into his home, he gets in touch with the overwhelming and universal love of God. He realizes and believes God's love applies to him, no matter what anyone else might say to the contrary.

Take Jesus into your most private places, and you, too, will discover that God's love is for you.

Fifth, dare to respond extravagantly to the love of God. The formerly blind man leaves his hometown to follow Jesus, though he does not have a clue where Jesus is going. Zacchaeus gives away one half of his wealth to the poor, and he promises to return any defrauded money at more than the expected rate. I think it's safe to call each response extravagant.

When we experience the grace of God at our point of deepest need, we are empowered to lay caution aside and throw in our lot with God in astonishing ways.

Sixth, dare to invest what the Lord gives in the service of the Lord. Luke wraps up the section by sharing his version of the Parable of the Talents.

A nobleman leaves his own country to go to the king, whom he hopes will grant him royal authority. Before leaving, he summons ten slaves, distributes ten talents among them, and tells them to invest the money.

The nobleman wins his case, returns home, and summons his slaves to give account of their investments. One slave's investment yields a ten-fold increase, another's yields a five-fold increase. One slave, though, hides his talent beneath a cloth because he is afraid he might lose it and suffer his Lord's wrath.

The nobleman reacts strongly. He takes the talent from the fearful slave and gives it to the one with ten talents, for he approves of those willing to risk loss in his service.

We, no doubt, can read many meanings into the parable, but here's what I think it means for those of us who intend to journey on the road with Jesus: never forget that all you are and all you have is a gift from the Lord Jesus. Throw yourself and all you have into the Lord's work.

And what is the Lord's business? Go back and read Luke 4:18-19: "The Spirit of the Lord is upon me, because he has anointed me to bring good news to the poor. He has sent me to proclaim release to the captives and recovery of sight to the blind, to let the oppressed go free, to proclaim the year of the Lord's favor."

There we have it—six lessons that, when taken to heart, help us get on and stay on the road with Jesus.

Let's hit the road.

41

Three Warning Signs of Unhealthy Religion

Luke 19:28–20:19

Do you ever skim headlines on the Internet? When the mood takes me, I do.

Headlines are written to catch our attention. They may or may not have much to do with an article's actual content. A headline's success is gauged not by its accuracy but by how many people it entices to click and read further.

Headlines tied to medical research and advertisements are among the most intriguing. We can't scroll long without encountering headlines such as the following:

Four Signs of Heart Disease
What Your Feet Are Telling You about Diabetes
Eight Signals Your Liver Is Sending You

You get the point. Headlines related to medical concerns grab our attention because most of us harbor questions about our health or the health of someone else.

While I place little trust in such headlines, I realize we need to know how to recognize symptoms of developing health problems. The sooner we discover, define, and deal with a health issue the better!

Much the same is true with regard to religion. How do we know when our religion is starting to become unhealthy? What are some of the signs?

Luke 19:28–20:19 points to three signs of unhealthy religion.

First, unhealthy religion attempts to silence truth. Jesus enters Jerusalem riding on a colt. People spread their cloaks on the road before him. His followers start to shout and declare him to be the promised Messiah, the king who comes in the name of the Lord.

Some (not all) of the Pharisees in the crowd object. "Teacher, order your disciples to stop!" (19:39). Jesus responds, "I tell you, if these were silent, the stones would shout out" (v. 40). In other words, Jesus regards what the disciples are saying as truth that cannot be suppressed.

Why did some Pharisees try to silence the truth? Let's be fair. Most likely, they deeply believed they were doing the right thing.

Some, no doubt, simply did not believe Jesus to be the Messiah. In their mind, he did not fulfill their understanding of the Scriptures, provide the required proofs, or observe the law in the right ways.

Others, I suspect, blended pragmatism with their religion. Even if Jesus was the Messiah, public shouting and large crowds might bring down the wrath of Rome. Such Pharisees might have harbored hope that Jesus would prove to be the Messiah, but they also dreaded the potential social and political fallout.

Let's not be too hard on the Pharisees. After all, Christians sometimes try to silence truth in the name of religion.

When I was a child, I listened as a Baptist deacon argued from the Scriptures that people of color were inferior to whites, segregation and discrimination were ordained by God, and all efforts to eliminate racism ran counter to God's plan. He urged us to silence those in our congregation who thought otherwise. Truth to tell, he tried to silence me.

For the first time in my life, I recognized the existence of unhealthy religion in my own time. Since then, I've encountered it again and again. Always it demands our silence in the face of injustice. "Tell your people to be silent about the full equality of women and men in the life of the church and the world." "Tell your people to be silent about God's insistence that we treat all people as we ourselves wish to be treated." No doubt you can provide other examples.

Second, unhealthy religion commercializes the faith. Jesus enters the temple grounds and begins to drive out those who are selling things there. What are they selling and who are their customers? They sell services and merchandise to Jewish people who come to the temple to worship. Many sell animals for sacrifice; others exchange temple currency for whatever currency worshipers might have on them. All these services turn a profit! Jesus calls the merchants "robbers," implying at the very least that they take advantage of the piety of their customers.

Temple authorities have long-standing arrangements with the merchants. No doubt a portion of the profit goes to the temple coffers. Both
the merchants and the temple authorities believe they offer a vital service to
worshipers. They think of themselves as the good guys.

That being the case, the temple authorities naturally confront Jesus.
How dare he denounce the financial and service structure they operate to
support worshipers and the temple? Jesus refuses to answer the question.
He leaves it up to those observing the scene—then and now—to determine
who is right about the matter.

What do you think?

When some media preachers accumulate personal estates worth mil-
lions of dollars from their followers' donations, what do you think? Might
unhealthy religion be in play?

When a person mired in poverty sends a donation to a ministry in
exchange for a prayer cloth and the promise that the cloth will bring with it
a blessing, what do you think? Might unhealthy religion be in play?

When a church evaluates its success on the basis of taking in more
money than it spends, what do you think? Might unhealthy religion be in
play?

*Third, unhealthy religion acts as if the faith belongs to it rather than to
God.* Jesus tells a parable about tenants of a vineyard who try to wrest own-
ership of the vineyard from its owner. As Jesus puts it, they reject and abuse
the owner's messengers. Finally, the owner sends his son to call them to
their senses and collect his share of the vineyard's harvest. The tenants,
though, kill the owner's son and claim the vineyard for their own.

At first the religious leaders don't realize the parable is about them.
When at last they get the point, they are angry with Jesus and wish to do
him harm.

Such behavior is not limited to the first-century world. For example, a
family in a small rural congregation in Indiana came to believe the congregation belonged to them. One family member served as treasurer, another
wrote checks and handled all church publications, and yet another taught
the only Bible study class for adults. Together, they determined the church's
budget, who might use the buildings, the elements of pubic worship, and
the structure of the church's ministries.

No doubt they started doing so with the best of intentions. Over
decades, though, they created a congregation in their own image. Their
extended family felt at home there, but, increasingly, others did not.

Eventually the church called a pastor who gently but persistently urged the church to acknowledge that it belonged to God and to act accordingly. The leading family became unhappy, challenged the changes, and was quite surprised when the rest of the congregation opted for a new way of being the church.

Whenever we start to believe and act as if the church belongs to us, we inevitably make the church over in our own image and wind up denying it belongs to God.

There's a better way, of course. We summarize it in the call to seek first the kingdom of God, which we Christians do best by following Jesus. For many of us, the way to spiritual health begins the day we acknowledge we've got a bad case of unhealthy religion and decide to do something about it.

42

Questions

Luke 20:20-44

Do you ever read a piece of Scripture and find yourself wondering why it found its way into the Bible? Why did the author believe this was important to record? How can it possibly apply to us in our time, an era far removed from biblical times?

I think quite a few Christians experience such thoughts when they deal with the three questions found in Luke 20:20-44. Let's see if we can unpack the passage and find meaning in it.

The first question focuses on paying taxes. Jesus is dealing with the scribes, experts in the law who generally are in league with the temple authorities. They have a vested interest in keeping peace with Rome. On the positive side, many of them want to avoid the kind of violence Rome visits on those who oppose it. At the personal level, some of them want to hold on to their privileged position in Jewish society, and the only way they can do so is to cooperate with the Romans.

According to Luke, they engage Jesus in conversation in an attempt to trap him with a politically sensitive question wrapped in religious language. The question is, "Is it lawful to pay taxes to Caesar?" (v. 22). That is, does it honor or dishonor God to pay taxes to the Romans?

If Jesus answers yes, he risks losing the support of many of the Jewish people. If he answers no, he leaves himself open to charges of insurrection against Rome. Either answer works to the advantage of the scribes.

"Show me a denarius," says Jesus (v. 24). In a neat twist, Jesus forces the scribes to show that they carry Roman coinage. By carrying and using the coins, the scribes reveal that they recognize the authority of Rome in their lives. Jesus then tells them to render to Caesar what belongs to Caesar and to God what belongs to God. His words are both direct and subtle. They are direct in that they admit Caesar has an appropriate place in human affairs. Each person must decide what that place is and act accordingly. His words are subtle in that by pointing to the image of Caesar on the coin he reminds them (and us) that all people are made in the image of God. All should render their lives unto God. The state has its place, but it must never take the place of God.

And the scribes are silenced, at least for the time being.

The second question is framed by Sadducees, the leading members of the priestly caste. They are supporters of the temple who accept only the first five books of the Bible as Scripture. The Sadducees reject the authority of the oral tradition, the Writings, and the Prophets. They, unlike the Pharisees, believe not in resurrection but in an older concept, namely that this life is the only life. Call them the "conservatives" of their day.

Their question attempts to ridicule the idea of resurrection by posing a comical hypothetical situation. Drawing on the practice of a brother marrying the childless widow of his brother as an act of obedience to God, they posit a situation in which one woman winds up married in sequence to seven brothers over the course of her lifetime. They then ask, "In the resurrection, therefore, whose wife will the woman be? For the seven married her" (v. 33).

Jesus ignores the question. In doing so, he treats it as too silly to be taken seriously. Rather than answer the question, he simply affirms the reality of resurrection. He adds that the resurrection life is a new kind of life beyond the reach of our imagination, one in which old questions pass away. It is a mystery to be experienced rather than explained.

Adding insult to injury, Jesus makes use of the Scriptures of the Sadducees to support the hope of resurrection. He notes that Moses speaks to God as the God of Jacob and does so in the present tense. Drawing on rabbinic methods of Scripture interpretation, Jesus concludes that Jacob must somehow be alive to God and, therefore, resurrection is real.

The Sadducees can do nothing more than acknowledge that Jesus has spoken well (v. 39).

Jesus poses the third question to the Sadducees: "How can they say that the Messiah is David's son?" (v. 41).

Jesus now takes the initiative. He has entered Jerusalem in a manner designed to lay claim to the role of Messiah. Jesus is keenly aware of the predominant conception of the Messiah, which teaches that the Messiah will not only be a descendant of David but will also replicate the feats of David. The Messiah, according to this scenario, will conquer the enemies of the Jewish people and establish an earthly kingdom similar to that of David.

Jesus uses Scriptures from the Psalms attributed to David to debunk such a notion. In the passage Jesus quotes, David depicts God saying that David's "Lord" is to sit at the right hand of God (vv. 42-43). Jesus then asks, in essence "How can David call someone who is only his descendant 'Lord'?" (v. 44).

His point is simple: the Messiah will transcend all expectations; the Messiah will not replay the life and rule of David but instead will do something new and unexpected.

The story of the three questions prompts me to ask myself some questions.

Have I fallen into the trap of framing religious and political questions in terms of yes and no answers? If so, might I need to reconsider my approach in light of Jesus' response to the scribes?

Do I primarily use religious questions and even Scripture to try to win theological debates and paint my position as the only scriptural perspective? If so, how do I think I might fare if I tried such an approach with Jesus?

Have I consciously or unconsciously tried to tell Jesus who he must be and what he must do with regard to the world, others, and even me? Do I really believe Jesus can be tamed in such a fashion?

Maybe it's time we focused less on providing answers and spent more time asking good questions.

What do you think?

43

Why Am I Religious?

Luke 20:45–21:4

Sometimes I wake up in the middle of the night and wonder why I'm religious. Blame it on our religious heritage. After all, we come from a religious tradition that encourages us to examine the motivations for all we do. Perhaps we go overboard sometimes, but for the most part I think it's healthy that we dare to ask why we do what we do, not least of all when it comes to religion.

In my own case, I ask, why do I publicly identify with Christ and the church? Why do I live the life of a pastor and writer? Why do I support the church and other endeavors with financial gifts, my time, and my influence? Do I do what I do because of God's call on my life or for other, more self-serving reasons?

Luke 20:45–21:4 supports such self-examination.

Start with the scribes. The scribes were religious professionals trained as skilled interpreters of the law. Their mission in life, in theory, was to help God's people discover, understand, and implement God's intentions in their individual and community lives.

Let's admit that some scribes took the mission seriously, immersed themselves in their work, and did so with little thought of personal reward. That being said, Jesus (and many others, no doubt) knew of scribes who used their position to feed their egos and build personal wealth.

Jesus paints a word picture. Such scribes rise in the morning, dress in their official clothing, and go walking in the marketplace. So far, so good. Isn't it wonderful that the scribes make themselves readily available to the people? The problem is that the scribes in question are out in public not to make themselves accessible to those who need them but instead to enjoy having their official status acknowledged via the respectful greetings of the people.

Jesus adds to the theme by noting that they use their office to justify taking the best seats in the synagogues and places of honor at banquets. When they pray in public settings, they fashion long, elaborate prayers, not for the purpose of placing themselves at God's disposal but in order to impress those listening. In short, such scribes abuse their profession in order to enhance their social status and clout.

More darkly, some of the scribes, while professing devotion to God's law and interpreting the law for others, flout it themselves. For example, while it is forbidden to take financial advantage of widows, some scribes fleece them of their resources.

Jesus concludes with a stern warning: such religious professionals will not escape God's judgment. The general principle is that those who misuse their position and religion to impress, mislead, or defraud others stand condemned in the eyes of God.

In similar fashion, Jesus notes a group of people dropping offerings into a receptacle in the temple. Anyone watching could discern large offerings from smaller ones. In this case, some rich people make their offerings. Perhaps they take their time, stretch it out, and make sure others have a chance to see the large gifts they give. At some point, a poor widow makes her offering as well, two copper coins, an amount so small as to have almost no buying power.

Jesus does not disparage offerings. Both the rich and the widow are engaged in the same act. In addition, Jesus is not arguing against the validity of public offerings per se. The temple provided a number of receptacles for receiving such offerings. It's even possible that each receptacle was designed for specific levels of giving. Perhaps the rich went to one to make their gifts while the widow went to another.

I like to think this is true. If so, it adds to the picture. In my mind's eye, I see the rich lined up at one place as the widow stands at another. All eyes in the temple track to the place where the rich toss in their offerings. Meanwhile, the widow goes unobserved by most. Surely her small offering is of no account in comparison to the donations of the rich.

But Jesus sees her and her offering, and he makes an astounding statement: "Truly, I tell you, this poor widow has put in more than all of them [the rich]" (21:3).

How can that be? What does Jesus have in mind? Just this: "For all of them have contributed out of their abundance, but she out of her poverty has put in all she had to live on" (v. 4).

I want to make it clear that Jesus is not saying the gifts of the rich don't matter. The money might actually wind up being well used. He is saying, though, that their gifts do not cost them anything significant or place them in the position of depending on God for their daily bread. Their gifts do not affect their financial security. Making such gifts confirms in the eyes of others that one is indeed rich. Some rich givers give in order to confirm their social status.

The widow, though, puts herself at risk by her giving. Let's put it in plain language. Her gifts are the rent and grocery money. In tossing the two coins into the offering bowl, she risks all she has and places herself in the hands of God.

And no one pays any attention to her. No one, that is, except Jesus.

Religious professionals and the rich—the elite of first-century Judaism—fail the test. While Jesus no doubt is painting with a broad brush, his point is clear: motivation matters. We get what we seek, and if position and influence and wealth are what we seek through the trappings of religion, that's all we'll receive.

God's approval is reserved for those who give of themselves because they think it is the right and trust-filled thing to do.

Like I said, sometimes I wake up at night and reflect on why I do what I do. And I hope you do, too.

I don't want to be or become a religious hustler, someone who uses the things of religion in order to boost my ego or line my pockets. And I don't want to be or become someone who enjoys the positive social payoffs of religion without it affecting my financial or personal lifestyle. Neither God nor the world needs another such religious imposter.

In my best moments, I want to be like the widow. I dream of being someone who chooses to trust God for everything so that I never hesitate to invest what I have in service to God.

I believe you do, too.

Such are the folk who nudge the world in the direction of the kingdom of God.

May you and I be found in their company.

44

What to Do when the World Falls Apart

Luke 21:5–22:6

I spend a great deal of time and energy interacting with fearful Christians. Truth to tell, I've lived so long with this situation that it's begun to feel normal. On my better days, though, I sense something awry. Why is it that we, the people of the one who tells us not fear, are so often afraid?

No doubt you could provide long lists of reasons for being afraid. A few years ago, I began to jot down a list of the fears I most often heard expressed. Even a partial listing suggests the range of our fears: nuclear war, job loss, economic depression, serious illness, terrorism (of various kinds and origins), Democrats controlling the nation, Republicans controlling the nation, biological warfare, social/political changes related to marriage, and—my personal favorite, submitted by a nine-year-old boy—shark attack.

Do you see a common thread running through all the items on the list? I do. Each involves a potential catastrophe that will undo our personal or corporate lives. We live in fear that our world, individual or societal, may fall apart.

Jesus often said, "Fear not," yet fear grips us, drives our decision-making, divides us into warring tribes, and generates yet more fear-inducing turmoil.

Luke 21:5–22:6 speaks a word of guidance to us when we are tempted to succumb to fear. We might not think this passage is helpful at first. It's filled with language about a besieged Jerusalem, signs and portents, and the like. Conditioned by more than a century of ill advised but well marketed end-time speculations, we mistakenly think the passage is concerned with the return of Christ.

It's not.

The very words of Jesus tell us the passage is about the decades between his own life and the destruction of the temple, for he says to those around him, "Truly I tell you, this generation will not pass away until all things have taken place" (v. 32). Jesus is warning his people that their world will fall apart in the space of a few decades. They will be tempted to deny the possibility, seek safety through flight, or take up arms to protect the life they know. And all such tactics will fail.

What, then, are Christ followers to do when the world as we know it falls apart? Jesus embeds pieces of counsel throughout his long speech.

He tells us to embrace a counterintuitive perspective: "Now when these things begin to take place, stand up and raise your heads, because your redemption is drawing near . . . when you see these things taking place, you know the kingdom of God is near" (vv. 28, 31).

God draws close to us, or perhaps we become more aware of God's presence, when the structures of life are shaken or destroyed. Those of us who follow Christ are called to look for God and what God is doing even in the darkest of times. I've heard such an assertion expressed by Christians living under persecution in Vietnam, an elderly woman fighting early-stage dementia, a man whose life savings were wiped out in the last recession, and a wife coping with her husband's infidelity. Each looked for and found God's presence in the circumstances, spotted something they thought God might be trying to do, and chose to move forward with God into whatever life might bring next.

Jesus is telling us to take the same approach as we wrestle with changes in the church and society in the early twenty-first century. The "temple" as we have known it (or at least as we perceived it to be) is coming down. We're tempted to see its demolition as the triumph of forces aligned against God. Suppose, instead, we choose to see God at work, deconstructing what we've known in order to clear the ground for what God would have come next?

Jesus took such a perspective. Let's join him!

What are Christ followers to do when the world as we know it falls apart? Jesus tells us to persevere in discipleship. He calls us to continue to follow him and do his kind of work in the world, even in a world in the process of deconstruction and reconstruction.

That's the point behind his talk about his disciples facing arrest, persecution by religious and civil authorities, prison, and the like. He tells his people to take such hardship as an opportunity to speak and act in ways that bear witness to the reality and character of Christ.

An acquaintance of mine was reared to become a religious terrorist. His father, uncles, and others trained him to believe he was on God's side in their war against all who did not share their religious perspective.

When he reached his mid-teens, they sent him to another country to receive additional military training. While there, he encountered an elderly Christian man who began to share portions of Luke's Gospel with him. The old man lived in constant danger of arrest, torture, and death. Yet he continued to follow Jesus, treat those who despised and persecuted him with gentleness, and share his faith. My acquaintance felt drawn to the Jesus the old man followed.

His world fell apart. His allies and family turned on him and threatened his life. For a time, he despaired. Eventually, though, he came to believe he could see God at work, taking apart his previous life in order to build a new one. He persevered. Today he is a Christian missionary, working among his people in India and Afghanistan.

Go and read today's text, and you'll find that Jesus follows his own advice. He goes about his business: praying, worshiping, teaching, and living out his particular ministry. He does so even as the temple authorities start to look for a way to seize him and put him to death. Even the developing betrayal by Judas cannot deter him.

I wish I could say we will never face times when our personal and social worlds fall apart, but all of us know better. The Bible doesn't promise that we or our cultures will enjoy a stable existence. Instead, we are called to discern God's hand in all things and remain faithful, even in times when our lives and the world are falling apart.

Let's choose to shift our focus from our fears to our faithfulness. Jesus calls us to settle for nothing less.

45

At the Table of Christ

Luke 22:7-38

I confess I used to be amazed at the company Jesus kept. Anyone could have told him he ought to have known better.

Here it was, the first Palm Sunday, the first day in the most important week in his life, and Jesus—not to be unkind, of course—was surrounded by the wrong kinds of people.

Take the twelve men, the ones nearest the donkey colt on which Jesus rode into the city. Jesus treated them as disciples, as devoted students who would learn from him and go on to be his face and hands and voice in the world.

Sometimes I just don't get it. He could have done so much better. Most of them were from Galilee, and everyone knew how Galileans were—Johnny-come-lately Jews, assumed to be troublemakers, clearly beneath Jerusalem standards, and given to speaking with an atrocious accent.

Even the handful of Judean folks in the group didn't amount to much. Matthew was a tax collector, a traitor to his own people. Judas might have worked with a group of insurgents before Jesus recruited him, and he may have been a bit of a thief as well.

None of them were outstanding disciples. They argued among themselves about who was the greatest, talked back to Jesus, and made promises they didn't keep.

As for all the people who vandalized trees and threw the branches before Jesus when he rode in on the donkey colt, they were a scruffy lot. Street rabble, that's how the authorities saw them. People with too much time on their hands and too little sense in their heads—the kind of folks who were so simple they still believed the Messiah might come. Such were the people who filled the streets and celebrated his entrance into the city.

I tell you, if I were Jesus, I would have found better people with whom to keep company, certainly better ones to bear my name. And I bet you would have, too.

I could have told him nothing good would come of running with such people. He held a Passover meal for the twelve. One of them, Peter, did some bragging at the meal, said something about being so brave and loyal that he would always stand with Jesus, even to the death. Another of them, Judas, left the meal, went to the priests, and sold Jesus out.

Here's another thing I don't get: Jesus saw right through them, saw that bragging Peter would turn into a quivering, Jesus-denying coward before the night was over, saw that Judas would betray him. How could Jesus, knowing them for what they were, invite them to eat his bread and drink his wine and call them family?

Once upon a time, that made no sense to me, no sense at all.

When I first learned that Judas brought the temple guard and some soldiers to the garden where Jesus was praying and tried to hand Jesus over, I wasn't surprised. What else would you expect of a man like Judas?

And when I read that Peter crept up to a fire outside the house where Jesus was being held and denied knowing Jesus, not once but three times, I was not surprised. What else would you expect of a Galilean?

When I learned that the others fled and hid and left Jesus all alone that night, I was not surprised.

Like I said, I could have told Jesus he couldn't count on such folk.

Yes, that's what I thought. That's what I thought until the day the Risen Lord paid a visit to me in the privacy of my heart. In that moment, I knew he saw right through me. I knew he saw each sin I had committed. I realized he saw each dark place in my imagination, each place I had ever been, each small and large betrayal I had committed, each occasion when I refused to say or do the right thing because I was ambitious or afraid.

I knew he saw right through me, yet he loved and welcomed me to his table anyway.

Suddenly I understood, and I was glad that Jesus had chosen to run with the wrong sort of people, people who—from his perspective—were just like me.

At last, I started to learn to take a place at the table alongside all the others from every place and every era, all the others whom Jesus saw through yet called his sisters and brothers, his family.

I began to eat and drink the food the Lord provides in the company of those I, too, now called my sisters and brothers in the Lord.

And it was good.

46

When Jesus Stood Alone

Luke 22:39–23:25

Jesus stands terribly alone during his last hours.

Though his disciples go with him to the Mount of Olives, he is alone as he prays and in the end says, ". . . yet, not my will but yours be done" (v. 42).

When Judas the betrayer arrives, Jesus stands alone in his reaction to the event. His disciples are not on the same page. They react with fear and violence. Jesus accepts the betrayal, reproves the use of counter-force, and submits to arrest.

For the rest of the night and the following day, Jesus stands alone. Most of his disciples flee. Even Peter, who once boasted of his loyalty to Jesus, keeps his distance and, when questioned, denies being a follower of Jesus.

Abused by the guards, rushed through a mock trial by the council, in Herod's court, and before Pilate, Jesus stands alone.

At last, Jesus is brought before the chief priests, leaders, and people of Jerusalem—the people of God, his family by blood and heritage. And they separate themselves from him, choose an insurrectionist over him, and call for his crucifixion. Pilate submits to their will, and he hands Jesus over to the soldiers who will crucify him.

Through it all, Jesus stands alone.

It seems to me that this tells us something about following Jesus. I don't like it (and I'll bet you don't either), but there are times when being true to one's self in God requires one to stand alone.

Most of us, I think, prefer company when we take risky actions in the name of God. Perhaps we think there's safety in numbers, or we need the assurance of knowing others agree with us.

But there are other moments, instances when we're the only ones on the scene to stand for the good, times when there's no one around or no one willing to stand with us. Such moments may come in any of life's settings.

Perhaps it's the workplace when we see a fellow employee being abused by an unhealthy compensation and rewards system. Perhaps it's when we witness the bullying or exclusion of an individual because of race, sex, illness, religion, or other features. Perhaps it's some other time or place where the majority goes against what we know is Christlike.

Jesus comes to a time when being the kind of Messiah he has chosen to be leaves him standing alone before the assembled powers of the world: politics, religion, economics, and self-interest. He chooses to embrace his isolation from other people, and by doing so he sets the stage for what God will do next. Followers of Christ must learn to expect and accept such moments to come their way.

God, preserve us from such moments of bitter isolation; God, give us the strength to accept and live into those moments if they come.

In the name of the Father, Son, and Holy Spirit. Amen.

47

"I Shall Die, and Remain Myself": The Death of Jesus

Luke 23:26-56

A friend of mine, a rabbi, teases that I cannot long go without referencing The Lord of the Rings series. He's probably right. Tolkien's great tale first gripped my imagination when I read it as an older child while homebound with an illness. I still reread portions of it each year, not least because I find a good bit of the gospel embedded in the story.

Take Galadriel, for instance. Like many of Tolkien's major characters, she faces the temptation to claim the One Ring, a ring that would give her the power to shape the world to her liking. All that is required is that she surrender all she has held dear and good.

She resists the temptation, refuses the One Ring, and declares, "I pass the test. I shall diminish and go into the West, and remain Galadriel."[1] Even as she does so, she knows the decision might mean her death and the destruction of her people and all her works. Hers is a hard and costly decision.

When first I read her tale, I found myself thinking of the death of Jesus. In the face of all possible alternatives, Jesus chooses to remain himself, the kind of person and Messiah he has chosen to be, even if doing so means death by crucifixion.

I've come to think that we should read the crucifixion account alongside Luke 4:1-21. In this passages, Jesus defines himself and his mission. Luke 4:1-13 features Jesus declaring what he will not be or do as the Son of God, the Messiah. In Luke 4:14-21, Jesus announces his embrace of Isaiah's vision for the Messiah. He will settle for nothing else and nothing less. Isaiah's vision leaves no room for a Messiah immune from suffering, death, or temptation.

Along the way to and while on the cross, Jesus continues to play out the great themes of his life and ministry. He pays attention to the weak and powerless. He counsels the women who wail for his fate, prays for those who are involved in his crucifixion, and welcomes the repentant thief to join him in Paradise. Even on the cross, Jesus continues to play the role of the Messiah who is God's good news to the poor, weak, sick, deluded, and sinful.

When noon arrives and the sky goes dark, Jesus places himself in God's hands, just as he has done all the days of his life.

Jesus remains true to the choices he has made. He does so in the face of a final temptation voiced by representatives of the political and religious leaders. They mock him and urge him to save himself if he actually is the Messiah, the Son of God. When I read their words, I hear echoes of the tempter's voice in the wilderness, the voice that urged Jesus to choose a safe way of being the Messiah that would preserve his life and win him followers.

Instead, Jesus chooses to remain himself, the kind of Messiah he has chosen to be, and to place himself and the results in the hands of God.

And he dies.

At that moment, it appears the world's powers have won. Where's the victory in dying? From their perspective, Jesus is a fool to believe love, humility, fidelity to God, and sacrifice can avail against the way of the world. They do not contest his burial in a grave provided by Joseph of Arimathea, for they believe his death ends Jesus' tale.

I find myself moved deeply by the death of Jesus, not because of the details of death by crucifixion but because of the depth of his trust in God. Jesus will die rather than live his life on any other basis.

When I grasp this, Jesus' words about discipleship take on added meaning. The phrases "Follow me" and "Take up their crosses" (Mt 16:24) become daunting.

Daunting yet liberating, too. For in Jesus, I see a new kind of human life dawning, a life re-centered in God. I see the possibility of each of us being remade, by the work of God in partnership with our own decisions, into people who follow the way of Christ.

Jesus remains Jesus as Jesus has chosen to be—even in the face of crucifixion and death. His is the way of full trust in God.

As it turns out, we can follow his lead and have his kind of life.
And that's good news, indeed.

Note

1. J. R. R. Tolkien, *The Fellowship of the Ring*, The Lord of the Rings (Ballantine Books: New York, 1965) 474.

48

We Are Easter People

Luke 24:1-12

Christ the Lord is risen, and I am an Easter person.

Yes, I believe Jesus was and is the Son of God . . .

. . . the one who willingly lived and died that all might be saved.

. . . the one who rose from the dead in triumph over the grave.

. . . the one who now dwells at the right hand of God as Lord of all.

. . . the one who will come again in God's time to end the age and launch a new heaven and a new earth.

Christ the Lord is risen, and I am an Easter person.

Because Christ is risen, I believe death has lost its sting, that when I die I shall step into the presence of the living Christ to dwell forever with him. And with the transformation of death from final enemy to servant of the Lord, I believe I need not fear to live here and now for Christ in the world as it is, for he holds me in his hands and shall not turn loose.

Christ the Lord is risen, and I am an Easter person.

Because of the resurrection, I know I am not bound to a meaningless life by my past, culture, or the deeds of others. The Risen Christ offers me a new life, his kind of life, and I have but to accept the gift in order to start to live that new life.

Christ the Lord is risen, and I am an Easter person.

I am one of many, both now and throughout history, of the Easter people of God. And I know in my heart that anyone may choose to believe and so come to know the forgiveness of God and the challenge and joy of living each day as an Easter person.

Oh, I believe Christ is risen. I, indeed, am an Easter person.

But I also know it is not always easy to believe.

Perhaps you know this, too. If so, be comforted. You are not alone. It has been so since the first Easter morning.

Imagine the night in Jerusalem before Resurrection Sunday. Many slept well that night. Pilate, Herod, the High Priest, many of the Council of Elders, the contingent of soldiers who had crucifixion duty, and the crowd of those who demanded the death of Jesus—all slept the night away convinced that the day had gone well.

Some did not sleep well. Eleven apostles plus uncounted women hid in a borrowed room. They passed the night in despair and in fear of what the morning might bring: temple guards, Roman soldiers, perhaps even a wooden cross for each of them.

In the dark of the night, they could not imagine a good ending to their story. Jesus, whom they had believed to be God's Messiah, had been executed as a rebel against Rome and a blasphemer against God. God had not saved him from the cross. The "world as it is" had won the day, and their hopes of a new world and new life lay buried in a borrowed tomb.

No wonder the men thought the women spoke nonsense that first Easter morning. They dared not believe the tale. Far wiser, they thought, to lay low until they could slip out of Jerusalem without attracting attention and go home to try to pick up the pieces of their former lies. Perhaps they should make peace with "the world as it is" rather than cling to false, foolish, and dangerous hope.

Even if they wanted to believe, they could not bring themselves to do so.

We understand, don't we? I do. It's not easy to believe Christ the Lord is risen when all around us "the world as it is" seems in charge.

We know what the "world as it is" looks like in action.

Somewhere last night a person died because of abuse, an untreated disease, or a fire in a poorly built structure.

Somewhere last night someone who should have lived instead died because "the world as it is" is callous.

Somewhere last night a woman cried herself to sleep because she had been beaten for speaking, for protecting her child, or for no reason at all. That's the "world as it is."

Somewhere last night a young person gave up all hope of getting ahead, defeated at last by poverty and economic systems beyond their comprehension. That's "the world as it is."

Somewhere last night someone died in despair, convinced that life is futile and death is the last word. That's "the world as it is."

Somewhere last night someone who had dreamed of the day when God's mercy and justice would flow down like a mighty river gave up the dream. Power groups, Internet gossip, high-paid pundits, threats, and worse wore them down and killed the dream. That's "the world as it is."

Let's be honest. Many slept well last night, deeply satisfied with "the world as it is." They slept soundly for they believed themselves to be on top of "the world as it is," and they felt comforted by the conviction that they would wake up to find nothing changed.

"The world as it is" is always with us, making it hard not to feel that God is absent at best and defeated at worst. Like the apostles and the others, we find it hard to believe that Jesus is risen.

Yet I believe Christ the Lord is risen. I am an Easter person.

The women in the story help me believe. Their story teaches me how to find and nurture belief.

They were the most powerless of the disciples, but they went to the tomb that first East Sunday without regard for the risk. They went out of love and duty. The women intended to honor the body of Jesus, to wash and anoint it with herbs, to give Jesus a decent, loving burial.

The women went to the tomb to do the only thing that lay within their power. They did the task at hand with no thought that doing so might land them in the middle of the resurrection drama.

Write it down. The women were the first to learn of the resurrection because they were the first to get up and get out, the first to do the deed at hand.

And they believed. In that moment at the tomb, they were transformed from simple mourners into apostles who bore witness to the good news of the resurrection and who became partners with God at work in the world.

Ah, there's the ticket! Could it be that we find it hard to believe because we're hiding in a room rather than getting up, getting out, and doing the deed at hand? The answer is yes. Belief springs to life most often in the midst of doing whatever we know of God's will, even something as simple as honoring the dead.

I believe, but I must tell you that my belief has taken shape and grown most often when I've chosen to try to partner with God.

My belief grows stronger each time I try to . . .

. . . build a world in which God's blessing is upon those who are poor, hungry, mourning, suffering for the sake of righteousness, loving even their enemies, turning loose of supposed safety in favor of trusting God.

. . . gather with others who worship the Risen Lord.

. . . die to life in "the world as it is" in order to be reborn to life "in the world as God would have it be."

. . . speak the good news that Jesus lived and died, was buried, and rose on the third day for the salvation of all.

. . . pray that others will acknowledge Jesus as Lord.

. . . intentionally yet humbly continue the mission of Jesus by becoming a friend to my fellow humans and living out the good news to all.

. . . call the mighty and the arrogant to repent and turn to God.

. . . allow myself to become someone in whom others might see enough of Jesus to be drawn to Jesus.

I have learned that my faith in the Risen Lord is sparked, nurtured, and matured by taking up the task at hand. Each time I do so, I become more nearly an Easter person.

We are Easter people. Yes, we know we have far to go. Yes, we know our failures of faith and nerve. Yes, we know "the world as it is" is still there and will be until the end of the age.

In spite of such realities, we are Easter people. The story that began that first Easter morning is not finished. It continues in us.

Christ the Lord is risen. I am an Easter person. You are an Easter person. We are Easter people.

In the name of the Father, Son, and Holy Spirit. Amen.

49

Walking with Christ

Luke 24:13-35

We often do not realize we are in the presence of Christ.

Two disciples were walking from Jerusalem to Emmaus. I suspect they had no conscious purpose for taking the journey beyond working off nervous energy. They almost certainly did not expect anything unusual to happen as they journeyed to Emmaus.

After all, they knew the seven-mile trip well. Perhaps they had walked it so often the scenery had become almost invisible to them. I would not be surprised to learn that they recognized the faces of some of the other travelers they passed on the way.

They were talking about all the things that had happened in Jerusalem: the last week of Jesus' life, his death, and the strange stories circulating about his resurrection.

It strikes me that they had yet to make a connection between all that had happened in Jerusalem and walking the familiar road to Emmaus. There was a disconnection. Jesus was on their minds, but they couldn't yet imagine that the resurrection had changed everything for them and the world at large. In spite of all Jesus taught them, the two disciples didn't yet see that Jesus was now with them at all times, in all places, and under all circumstances.

As they talked, a stranger caught up and walked with them. They thought nothing of it. This sort of thing happened from time to time on the road. There was safety in numbers! The stranger asked them what they were talking about, and that, too, seemed normal to them. Life was proceeding as usual there on the road.

The stranger drew them out. We, of course, know the stranger was Jesus. Luke treats us to the remarkable scene of Jesus leading the two disciples to tell him the story of himself. The stranger who was Jesus took over the conversation. He upbraided them and told them they were slow to comprehend that the prophets declared the Messiah would suffer such things before being glorified. He then went on to recast their understanding of the Torah and the prophets in light of Jesus' story.

Here's what interests me: the disciples did not recognize Jesus as he walked with them and expounded the Scriptures. No, indeed. Instead, hospitality prepared the way for recognition. They insisted the stranger stay the night with them, and he agreed.

Later, at dinner, Jesus took the bread, blessed it, broke it, and gave it to them. As Luke puts it, "Then their eyes were opened, and they recognized him" (v. 31).

Maybe the moment transported them back to the upper room and the supper Jesus instituted. Suddenly they were jarred from a mode of thought given to trying to fit the Jesus story into what they already knew of life. There at the table with Jesus, they were pulled into a worshipful way of seeing all things. Seeing Jesus, they realized he now was with them all the time. The resurrection, they now knew, had changed everything.

I try hard to remember the story of the two disciples who walked away from Jerusalem only to find that Jesus walked with them.

Why? The answer is simple. I want to see Jesus. I want to sense him as I go to and fro, walk the roads I choose to walk and even some roads I'm forced to walk.

Only I find it hard to do so more times than I like to admit. Don't you? Buffeted by life, I grow tired, and my eyes grow dim.

This story reminds me that Jesus is already there. He always catches up with me, walks beside me, draws me out, and helps me see how God is present and working in my neighborhood and the larger world.

Do you want to see Jesus? I hope so. Perhaps you and I would do well to start each day with a simple prayer: "Lord, I want to see you. Come walk with me and open my eyes!"

50

Open Your Mind

Luke 24:36-53

What are Christ followers to do between the resurrection and when this same Jesus comes again? The New Testament offers several answers, all of which call us to fill the time with Christlike, life-defining actions. I think the most challenging may be the Jesus-given mandate to open our minds.

Is your mind open or closed? That's a vital question these days, for we live in an era that tends to celebrate and reward closed minds.

This makes me think of a man I knew long ago.

Everyone in my hometown called him Old Man Shaw. Old Man Shaw never seemed to change his mind about anything. He was long-term member of our little Baptist church, a man who enjoyed praying in public, and a Sunday school teacher of seventh and eighth grade boys.

He was also a profound hater. Old Man Shaw hated people whose skin color differed from his own, people from Eastern Europe, women who thought themselves equal to men, stray dogs, and Democrats.

He read his Bible daily. I have to give him credit for that, for he knew the content of his Bible as well as anyone I've ever known. Truth to tell, he claimed the Bible was the only book he ever read. Old Man Shaw would never have used such language, but if he had, he would have said his entire view of life and the world was based on the Bible.

Actually, his perspective rested on his particular interpretation of the Bible, first taught to him as a child. He saw the world through a particular, and hateful, lens.

Old Man Shaw lived his life trapped in a closed mind. He paid the price for his closed mindedness, and he made a fair number of others pay as well.

He thought Jesus was proud of him. I suspect Jesus wept over him.

Jesus weeps over our closed minds because Jesus is about the business of opening closed minds so that we see everything in light of him.

The Scripture passage drives home the point. The Risen Lord comes to the disciples, takes hold of their worldview, and turns it upside down. He opens their minds so that they come to see all they've been taught and known in a new way, a way transformed and conditioned by Jesus.

Luke tells us Jesus took them through the Law of Moses, the Prophets, and the Psalms. It was not the first time they had taken such a trip. The Law, Prophets, and Psalms were their Scriptures. The disciples learned them well in the synagogue and their childhood homes. They memorized large portions of them and used them in worship, prayer, conversation, and debate.

The disciples knew the Scriptures, trusted them, and were shaped by them—or, at least, they knew, trusted, and were shaped by a given interpretation of their Scriptures.

They did not realize it, but their minds were closed, trapped in an interpretation loop so to speak, a loop on which they went round and round, always revisiting the same places, arguments, and conclusions.

Caught in the loop, they believed their Scriptures were mostly about how they were the chosen of God, how they were to keep their distance from Gentiles, and how God would someday make them powerful and safe from the rest of humanity. That's an oversimplification, but it's not far off the mark. Such was their worldview.

Jesus opened their minds to see their Scriptures in light of Jesus. In doing so, he set the stage for them to change their attitudes and behaviors in ways almost beyond belief.

Take Peter for example. Once he learned to interpret and weigh all Scriptures in light of Jesus, his opinion of Gentiles changed. Not easily, mind you. Months later, he experienced a vision in which God told him not to despise any creature God had made (Acts 10:9-16). Shortly thereafter, he found himself in the home of a Roman centurion, and he saw God working in the man's life. Peter, who had believed the Scriptures largely excluded Gentiles from God's care and fellowship with folk like him, changed his mind. He welcomed the centurion into the church, baptized him and his household, stayed in his home, and even ate with his family (Acts 10:44-48).

Peter endured hard questions and backlash from fellow Jewish Christians who did not see things as he did. But from that point on, with several starts and stops, Peter took the gospel to the Gentiles and thereby helped change the church and the world.

Can we imagine what modern pundits would say about Peter? They would accuse him of inconsistency, flip-flopping on the status of Gentiles, and abandoning the time-tested ways of God. Such pundits would try to read Peter out of the church, wouldn't they?

Like I said, we live in an era that tends to celebrate and reward closed minds. We're not unique. Peter lived in such an era, too.

All of this brings to mind a question: Who do we remember and celebrate today? Do we remember and celebrate those in the early church who resisted opening their minds to a new way of interpreting the Scriptures in light of Jesus? Or do we celebrate those who opened their minds and embraced a new worldview that led the church to break down religiously and culturally sanctioned prejudice, share Jesus with the full spectrum of humanity, and welcome any who chose to confess Jesus as Lord?

Who do we remember and celebrate? We know the answer, don't we?

Do we remember and celebrate those who cast off centuries of interpretative tradition in order to oppose child labor, slavery, segregation, and racism, or do we celebrate those who clung to interpretative traditions that endorsed such evils?

Who do we remember and celebrate? We know the answer, don't we?

We honor those who opened their minds to Jesus, embraced a Jesus-driven interpretation of the Scriptures, and so changed the thought and course of the church in the world.

Let's come back to Old Man Shaw. He lived his entire life in the church and with the Bible, but he never changed his mind about a single thing. And he died a bitter man. He died angry at his church, which slowly changed in spite of him to move a little closer to the Jesus way of seeing the world. He died angry at the larger society, which did some of the same. I suspect he died more than a bit angry with God for having failed to back him.

What a contrast to Peter, who according to legend died a horrible death yet was content to know he had taken on the worldview of Jesus and so felt blessed to suffer in the company of Jesus.

With whom will you and I be numbered? Will we open our minds so that Christ might change them, and in changing them reshape us into the kind of followers he desires?

Let us so pray, if we dare.